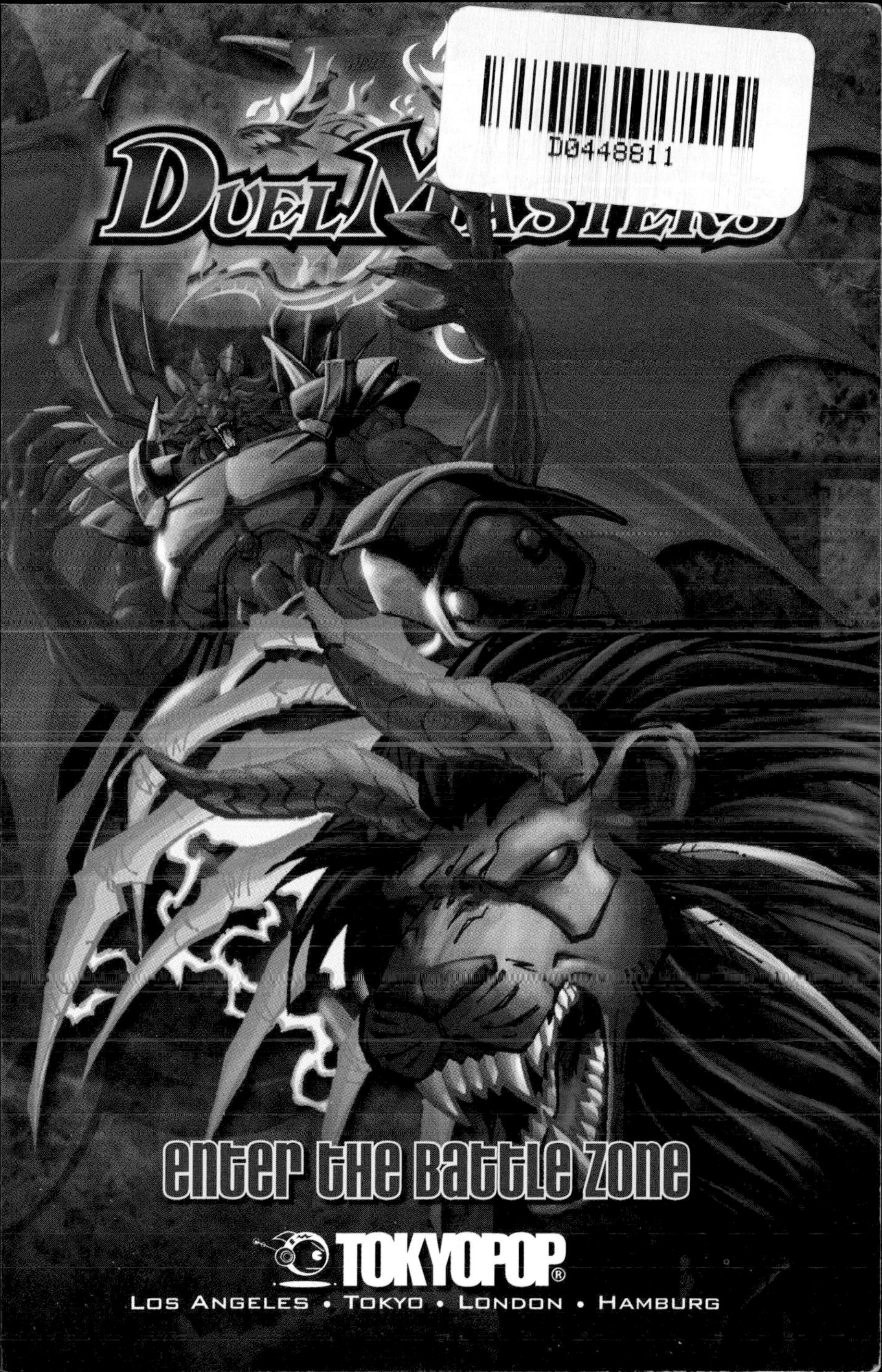
Duel Masters
enter the battle zone

TOKYOPOP®
Los Angeles • Tokyo • London • Hamburg

Contributing Editors - Amy Court Kaemon & Scott Reynolds
Graphic Design & Lettering - Monalisa J. de Asis, Jennifer Nunn-Iwai,
Tomás Montalvo-Lagos & Anh Trinh
Cover Layout - Raymond Makowski

Editor - Erin Stein
Digital Imaging Manager - Chris Buford
Pre-Press Manager - Antonio DePietro
Production Managers - Jennifer Miller & Mutsumi Miyazaki
Art Director - Matt Alford
Managing Editor - Jill Freshney
VP of Production - Ron Klamert
President & C.O.O. - John Parker
Publisher & C.E.O. - Stuart Levy

Come visit us online at www.TOKYOPOP.com

A  Cine-Manga™

TOKYOPOP Inc.
5900 Wilshire Blvd., Suite 2000, Los Angeles, CA 90036

Duel Masters Volume 1: Enter the Battle Zone

Wizards of the Coast and the Wizards of the Coast logo are trademarks of Wizards of the Coast, Inc.
Duel Masters and the Duel Masters logo are trademarks of Wizards/Shogakukan/Mitsui-Kids.
© 2004 Wizards/Shogakukan/Mitsui-Kids/Sho Pro. All rights reserved.
Original manga artist - Shigenobu Matsumoto.

All rights reserved. No portion of this book may be reproduced or transmitted
in any form or by any means without written permission from the copyright
holders. This Cine-Manga is a work of fiction. Any resemblance to actual events
or locales or persons, living or dead, is entirely coincidental.

ISBN: 1-59532-063-6

First TOKYOPOP printing: July 2004

10 9 8 7 6 5 4 3 2 1

Printed in Canada

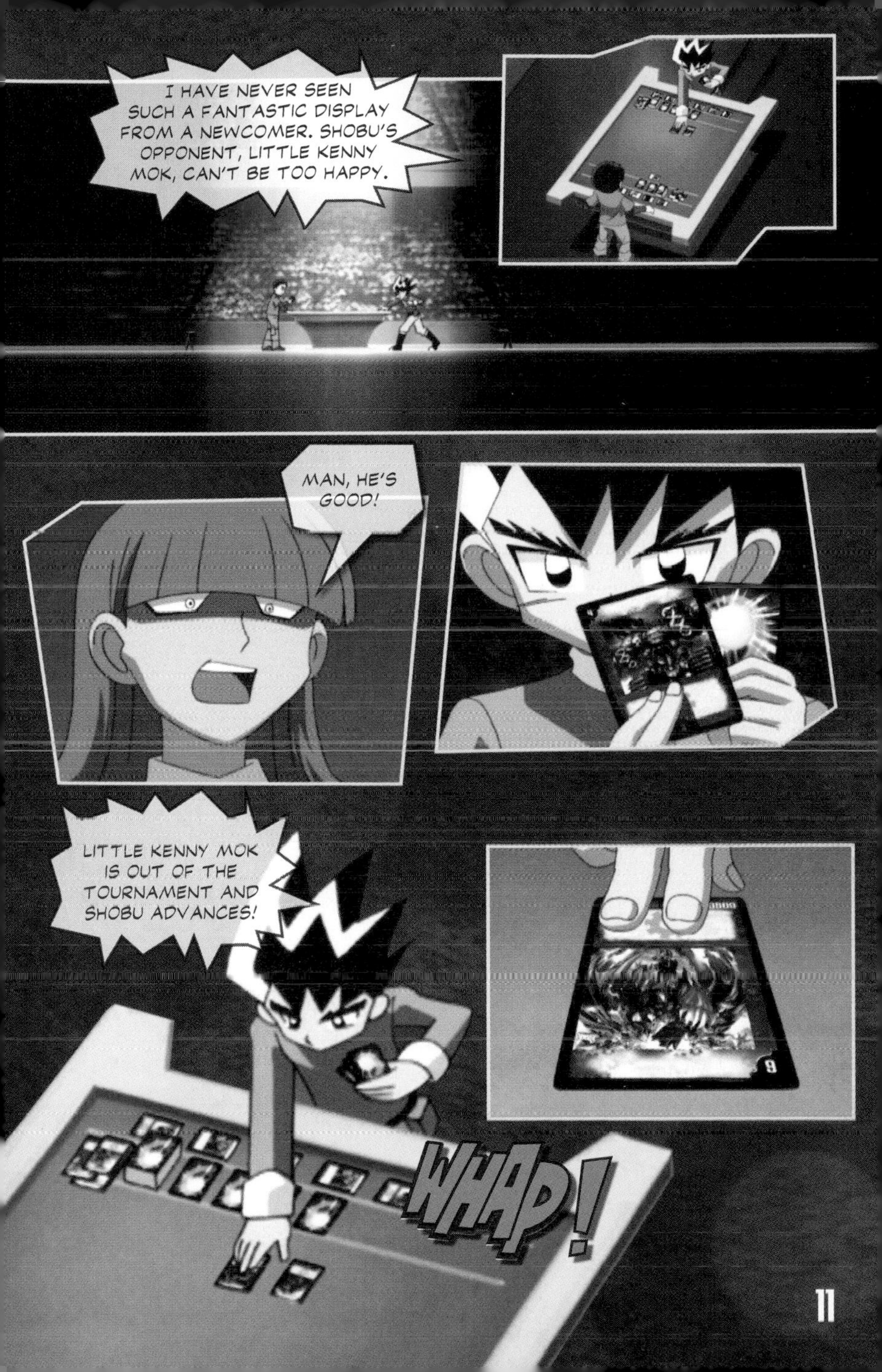
I HAVE NEVER SEEN SUCH A FANTASTIC DISPLAY FROM A NEWCOMER. SHOBU'S OPPONENT, LITTLE KENNY MOK, CAN'T BE TOO HAPPY.
MAN, HE'S GOOD!
LITTLE KENNY MOK IS OUT OF THE TOURNAMENT AND SHOBU ADVANCES!
WHAP!

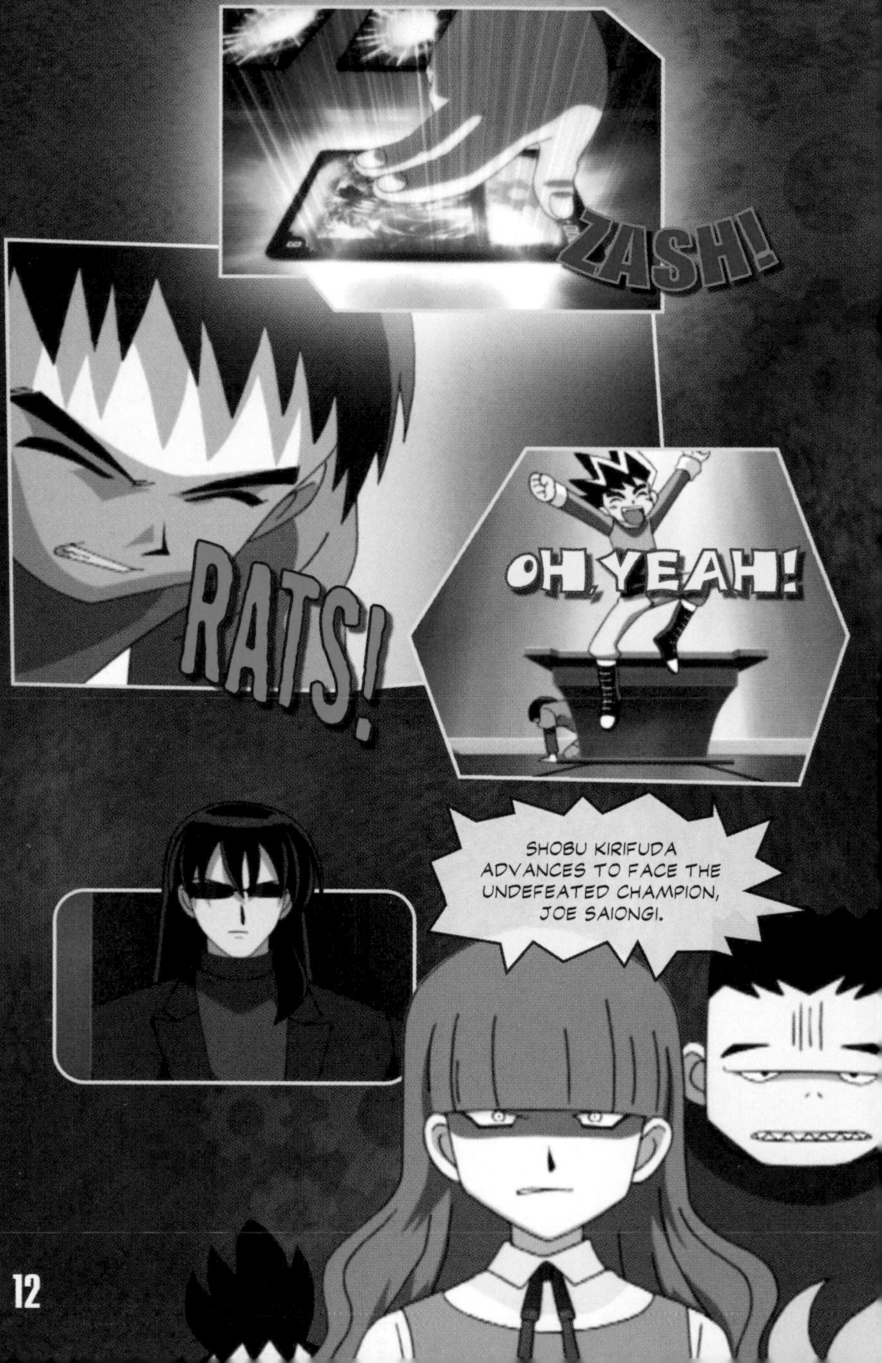
ZASH!
RATS!
OH YEAH!
SHOBU KIRIFUDA ADVANCES TO FACE THE UNDEFEATED CHAMPION, JOE SAIONGI.

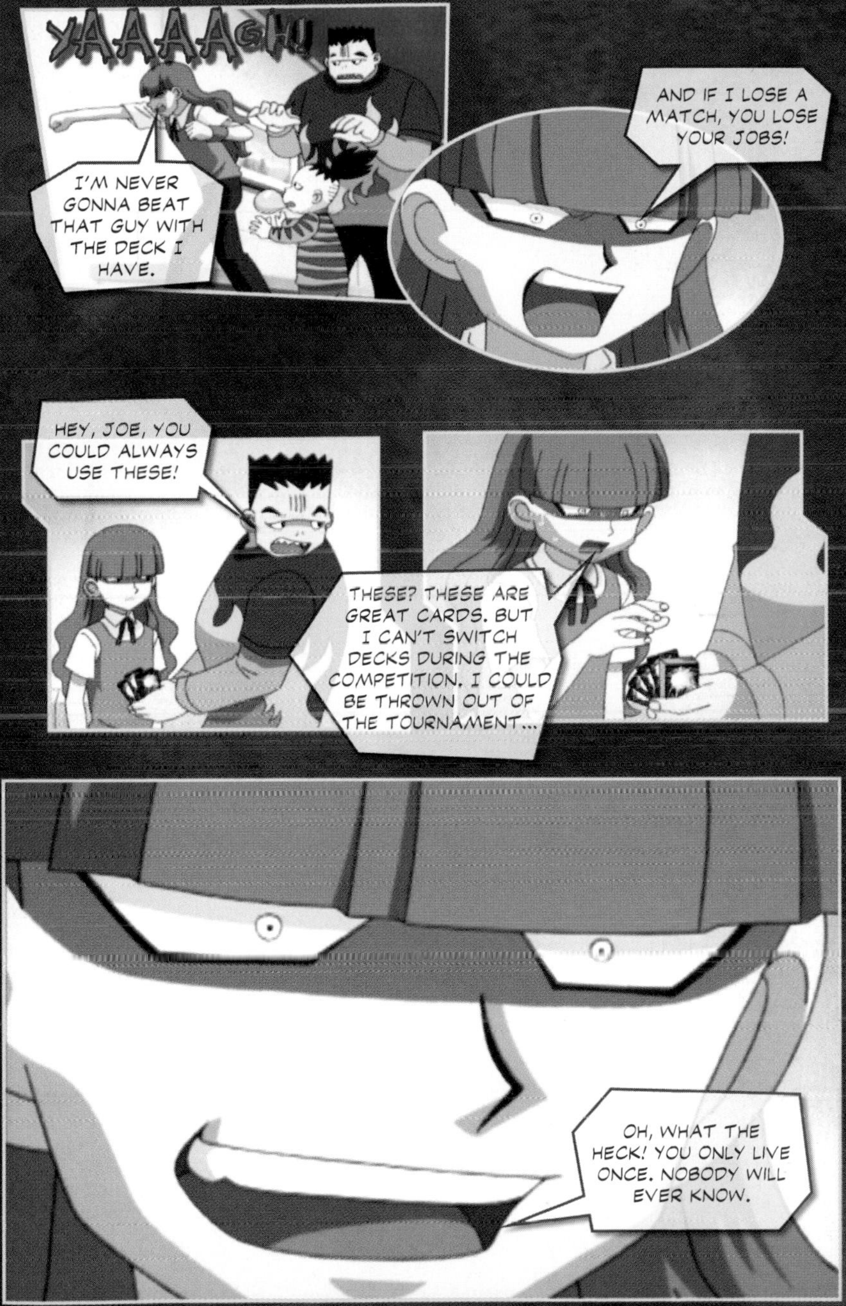
YAAAAGH!!
I'M NEVER GONNA BEAT THAT GUY WITH THE DECK I HAVE.
AND IF I LOSE A MATCH, YOU LOSE YOUR JOBS!
HEY, JOE, YOU COULD ALWAYS USE THESE!
THESE? THESE ARE GREAT CARDS. BUT I CAN'T SWITCH DECKS DURING THE COMPETITION. I COULD BE THROWN OUT OF THE TOURNAMENT...
OH, WHAT THE HECK! YOU ONLY LIVE ONCE. NOBODY WILL EVER KNOW.

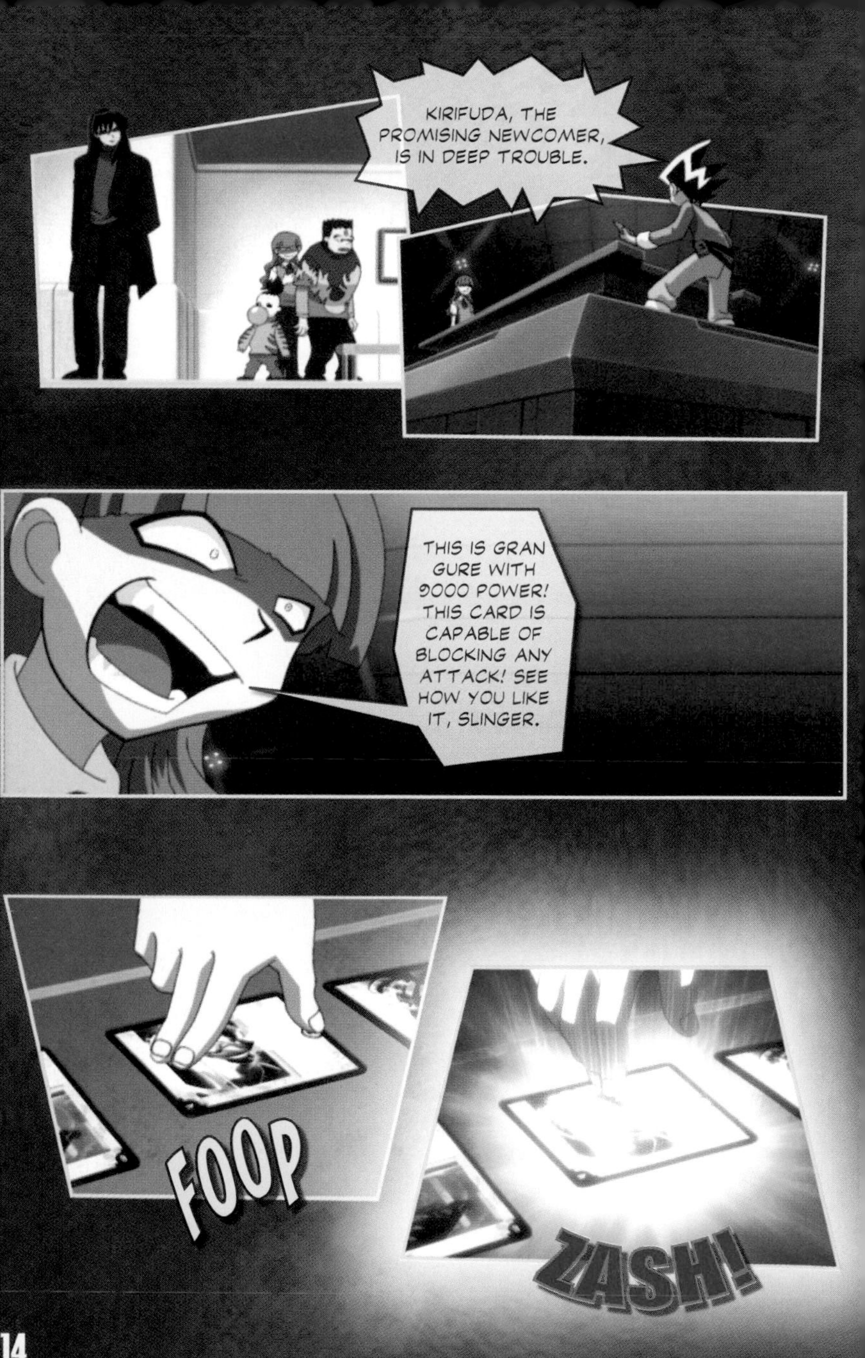
KIRIFUDA, THE PROMISING NEWCOMER, IS IN DEEP TROUBLE.
THIS IS GRAN GURE WITH 9000 POWER! THIS CARD IS CAPABLE OF BLOCKING ANY ATTACK! SEE HOW YOU LIKE IT, SLINGER.
FOOP
ZASH!

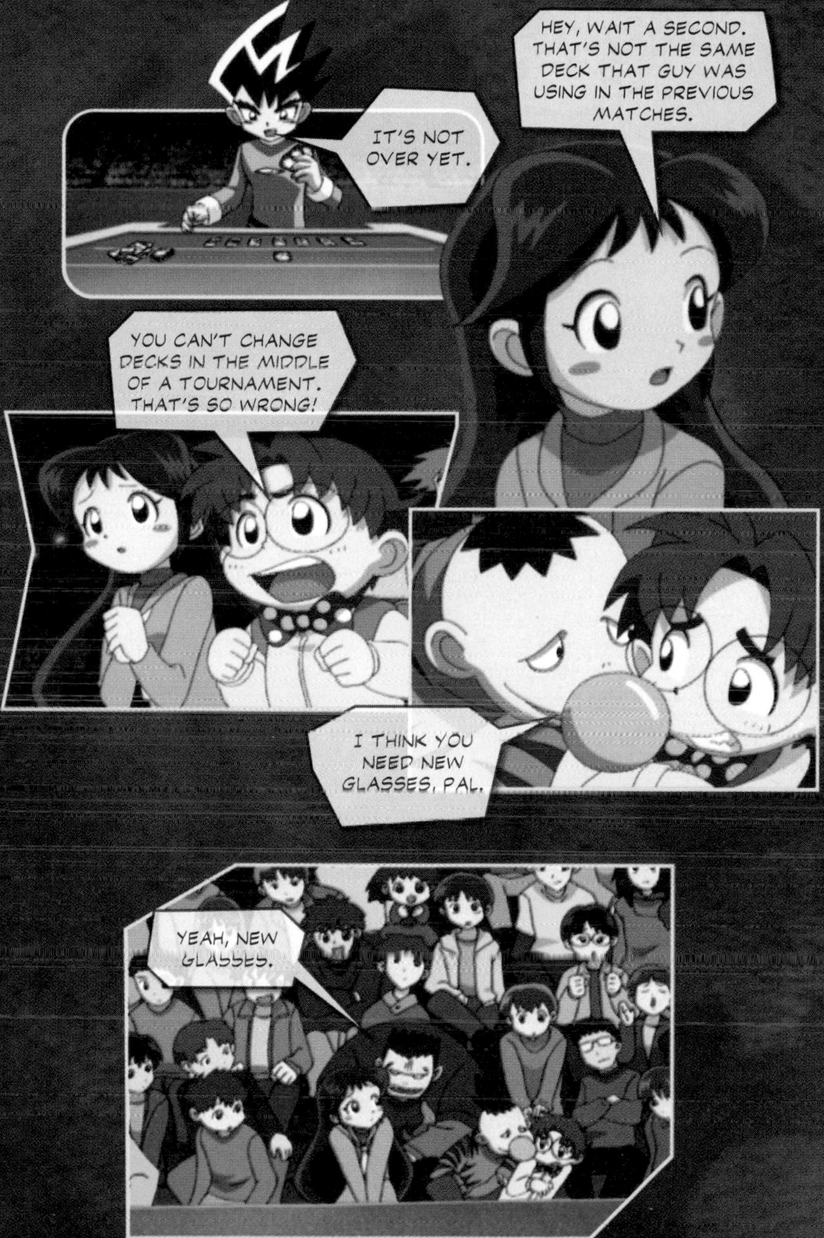

IT'S NOT OVER YET.
HEY, WAIT A SECOND. THAT'S NOT THE SAME DECK THAT GUY WAS USING IN THE PREVIOUS MATCHES.
YOU CAN'T CHANGE DECKS IN THE MIDDLE OF A TOURNAMENT. THAT'S SO WRONG!
I THINK YOU NEED NEW GLASSES, PAL.
YEAH, NEW GLASSES.

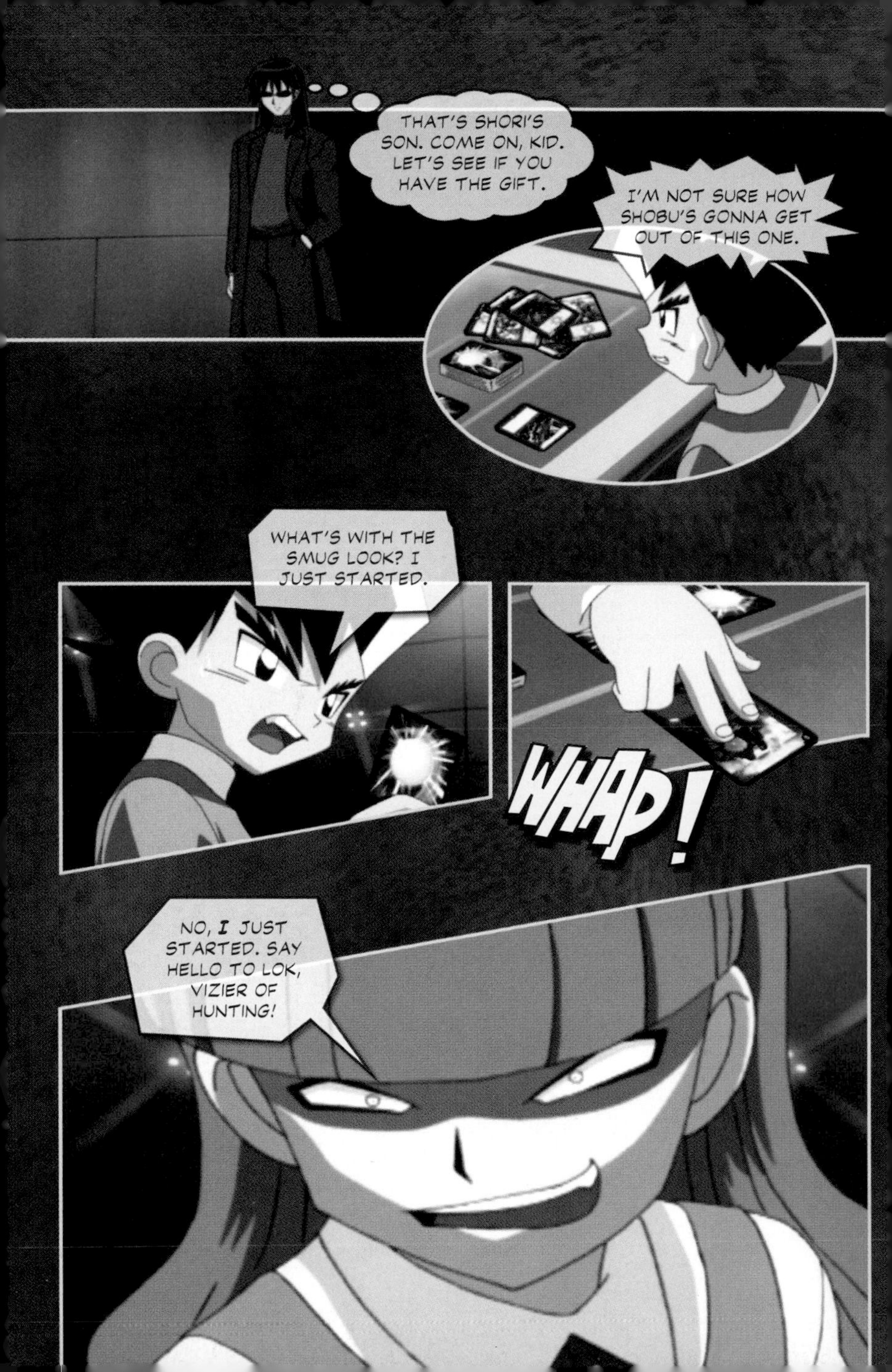
THAT'S SHORI'S SON. COME ON, KID. LET'S SEE IF YOU HAVE THE GIFT.
I'M NOT SURE HOW SHOBU'S GONNA GET OUT OF THIS ONE.
WHAT'S WITH THE SMUG LOOK? I JUST STARTED.
WHAP!
NO, I JUST STARTED. SAY HELLO TO LOK, VIZIER OF HUNTING!

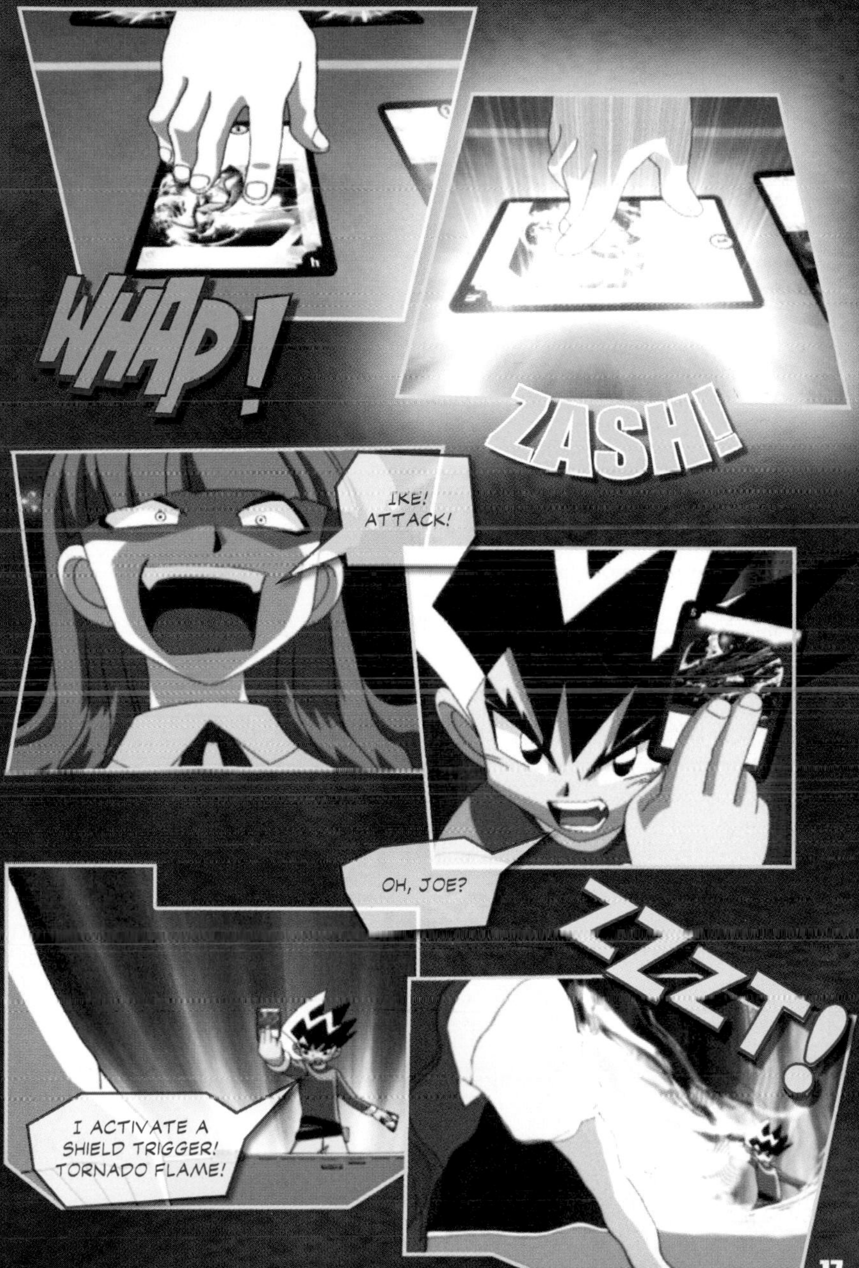
WHAP!
ZASH!
IKE! ATTACK!
OH, JOE?
ZZZT!
I ACTIVATE A SHIELD TRIGGER! TORNADO FLAME!

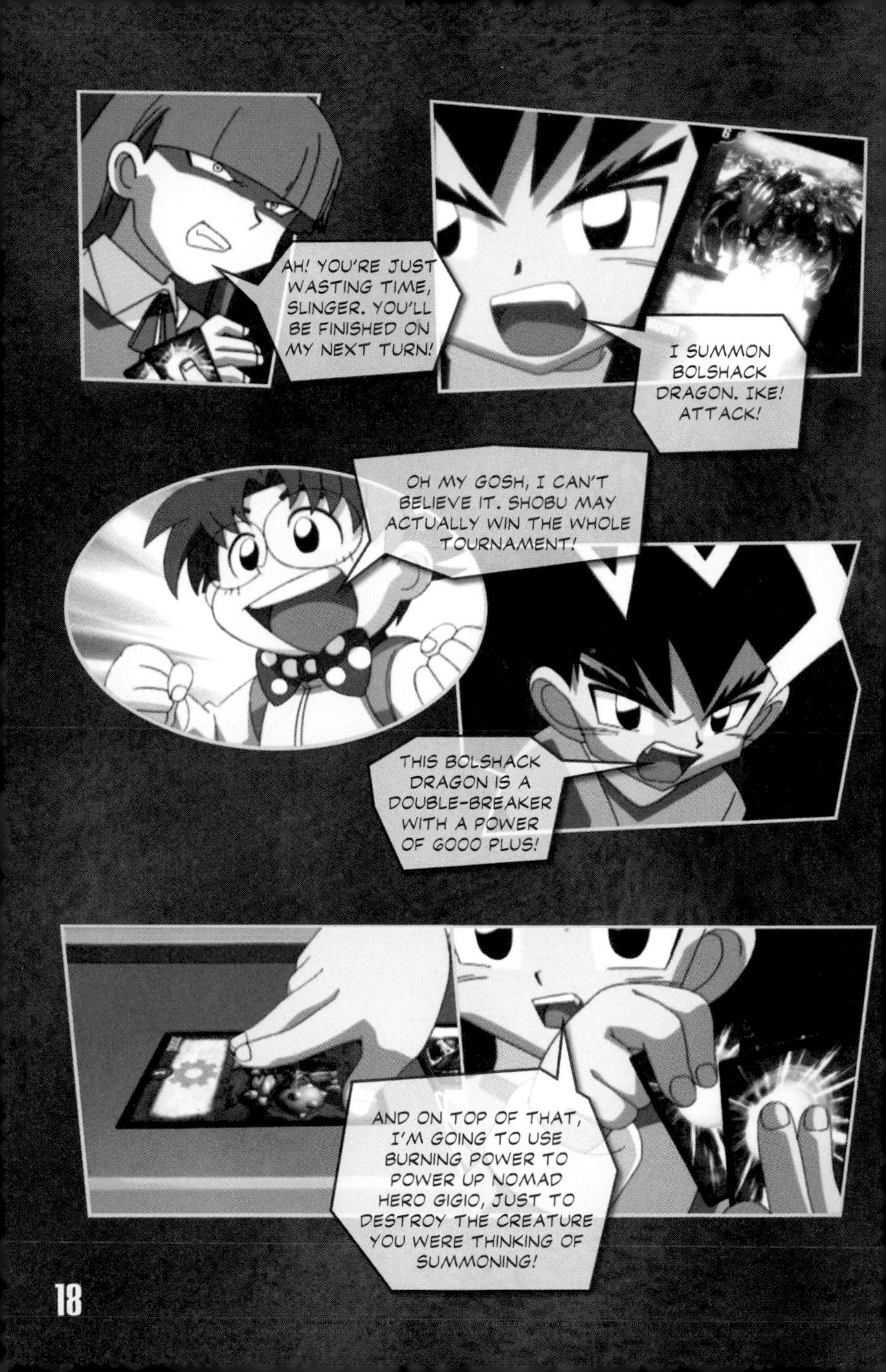
AH! YOU'RE JUST WASTING TIME, SLINGER. YOU'LL BE FINISHED ON MY NEXT TURN!
I SUMMON BOLSHACK DRAGON. IKE! ATTACK!
OH MY GOSH, I CAN'T BELIEVE IT. SHOBU MAY ACTUALLY WIN THE WHOLE TOURNAMENT!
THIS BOLSHACK DRAGON IS A DOUBLE-BREAKER WITH A POWER OF 6000 PLUS!
AND ON TOP OF THAT, I'M GOING TO USE BURNING POWER TO POWER UP NOMAD HERO GIGIO, JUST TO DESTROY THE CREATURE YOU WERE THINKING OF SUMMONING!

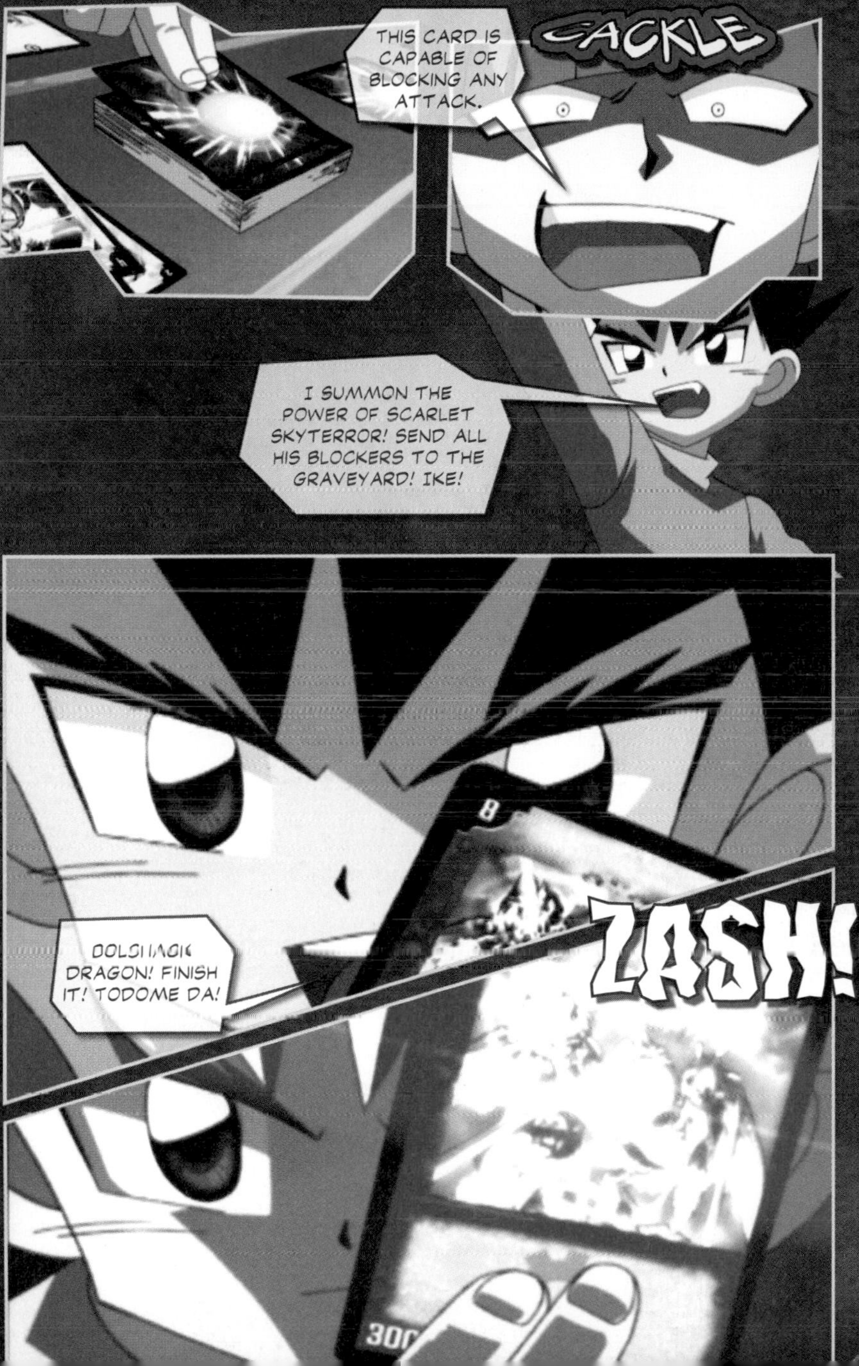
THIS CARD IS CAPABLE OF BLOCKING ANY ATTACK.
CACKLE
I SUMMON THE POWER OF SCARLET SKYTERROR! SEND ALL HIS BLOCKERS TO THE GRAVEYARD! IKE!
DRAGON! FINISH IT! TODOME DA!
ZASH!

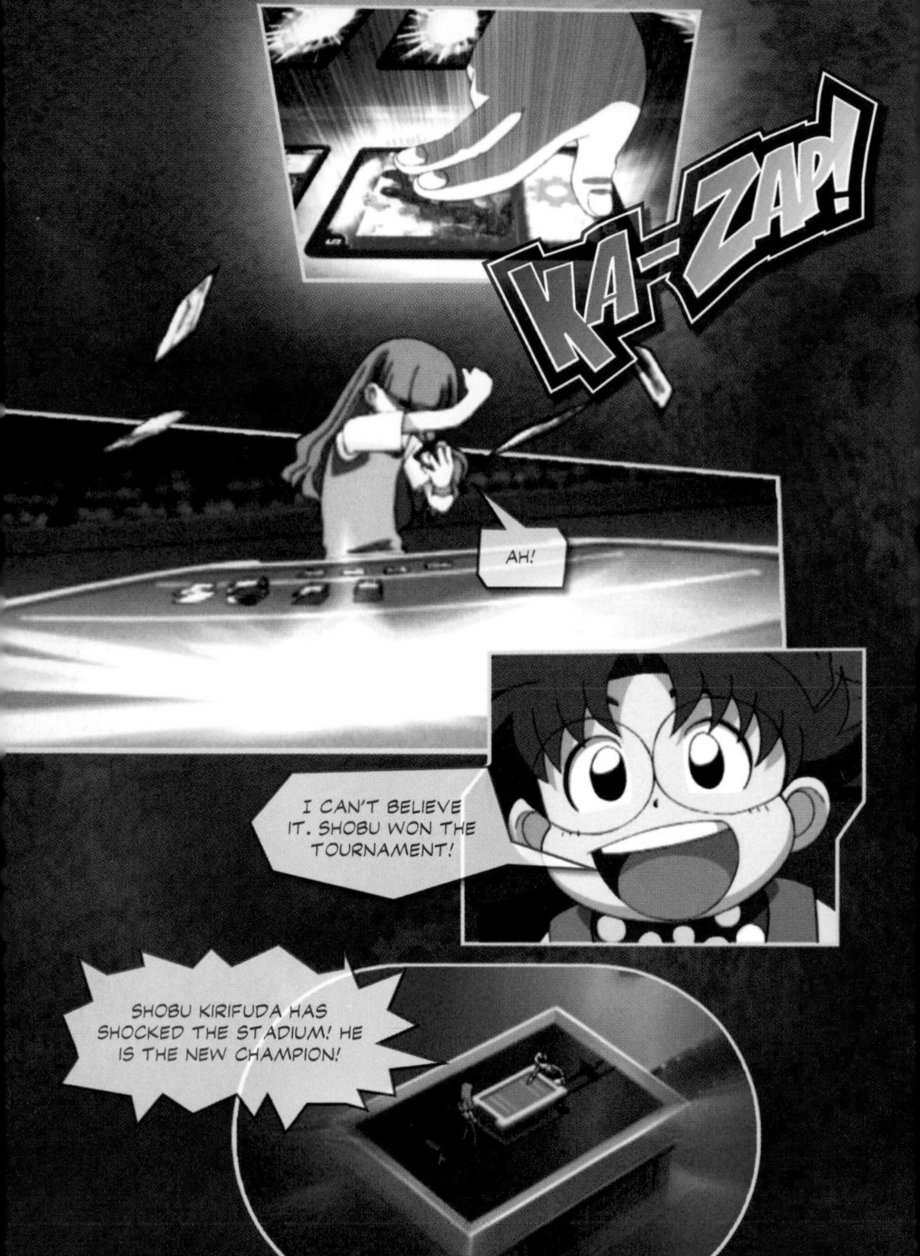
KA-ZAP!
AH!
I CAN'T BELIEVE IT. SHOBU WON THE TOURNAMENT!
SHOBU KIRIFUDA HAS SHOCKED THE STADIUM! HE IS THE NEW CHAMPION!

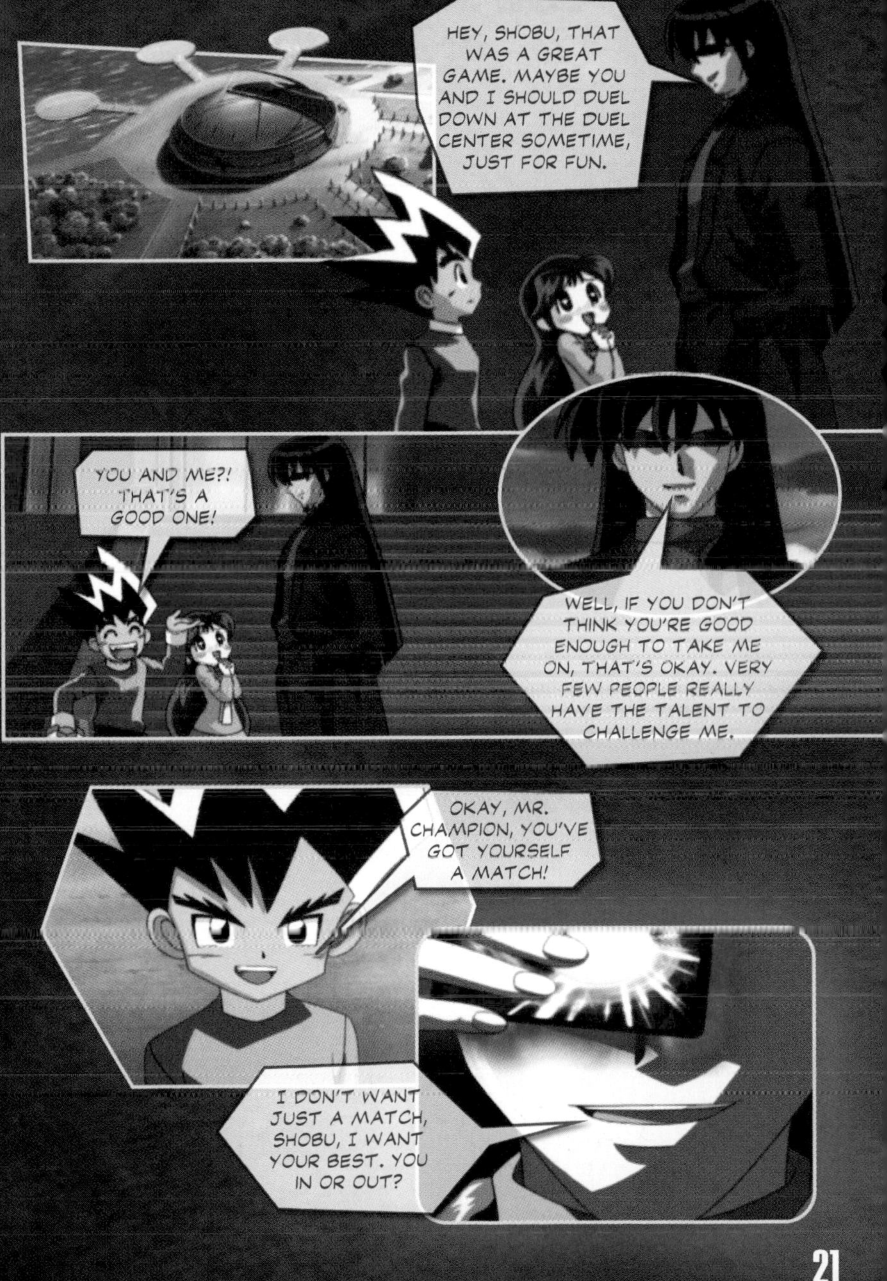
HEY, SHOBU, THAT WAS A GREAT GAME. MAYBE YOU AND I SHOULD DUEL DOWN AT THE DUEL CENTER SOMETIME, JUST FOR FUN.
YOU AND ME?! THAT'S A GOOD ONE!
WELL, IF YOU DON'T THINK YOU'RE GOOD ENOUGH TO TAKE ME ON, THAT'S OKAY. VERY FEW PEOPLE REALLY HAVE THE TALENT TO CHALLENGE ME.
OKAY, MR. CHAMPION, YOU'VE GOT YOURSELF A MATCH!
I DON'T WANT JUST A MATCH, SHOBU, I WANT YOUR BEST. YOU IN OR OUT?

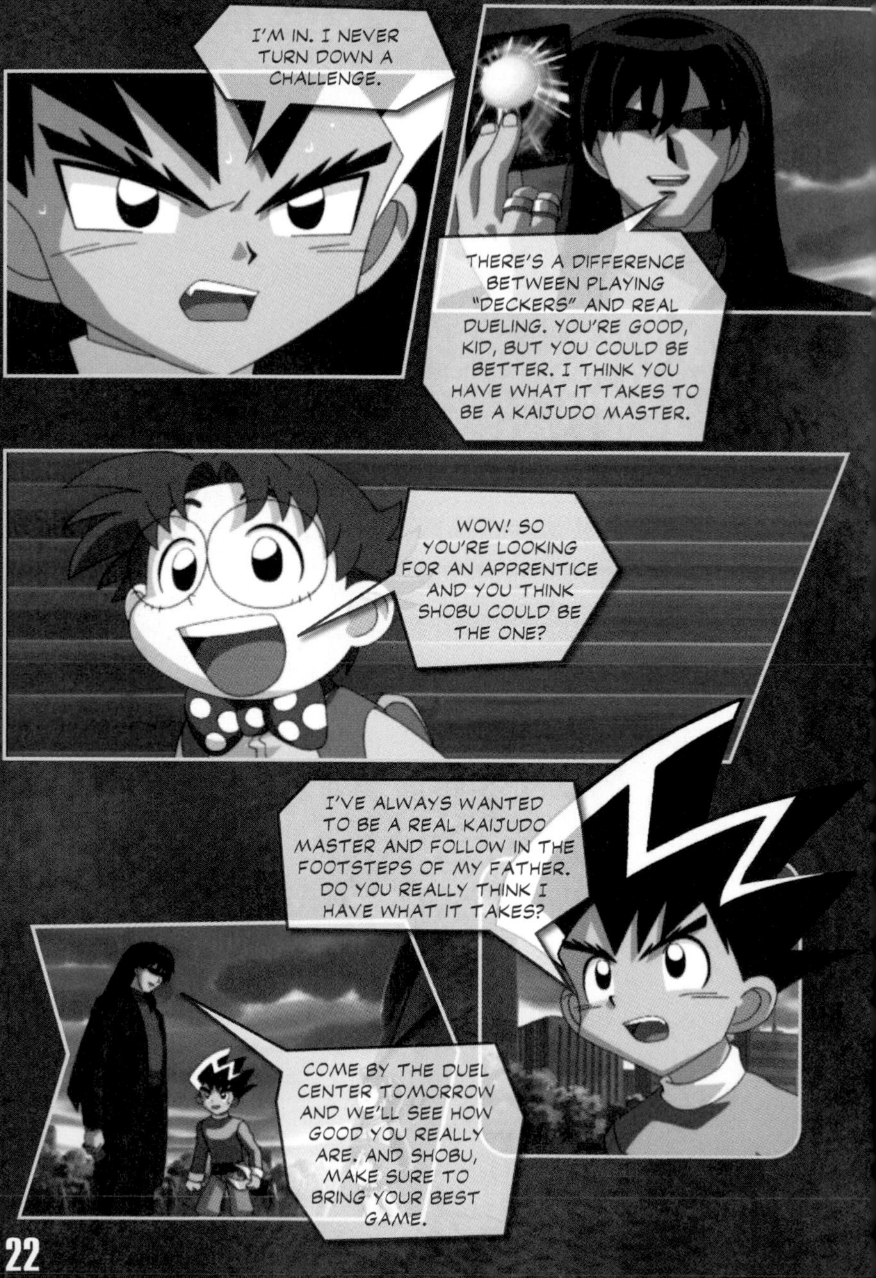
I'M IN. I NEVER TURN DOWN A CHALLENGE.
THERE'S A DIFFERENCE BETWEEN PLAYING "DECKERS" AND REAL DUELING. YOU'RE GOOD, KID, BUT YOU COULD BE BETTER. I THINK YOU HAVE WHAT IT TAKES TO BE A KAIJUDO MASTER.
WOW! SO YOU'RE LOOKING FOR AN APPRENTICE AND YOU THINK SHOBU COULD BE THE ONE?
I'VE ALWAYS WANTED TO BE A REAL KAIJUDO MASTER AND FOLLOW IN THE FOOTSTEPS OF MY FATHER. DO YOU REALLY THINK I HAVE WHAT IT TAKES?
COME BY THE DUEL CENTER TOMORROW AND WE'LL SEE HOW GOOD YOU REALLY ARE. AND SHOBU, MAKE SURE TO BRING YOUR BEST GAME.

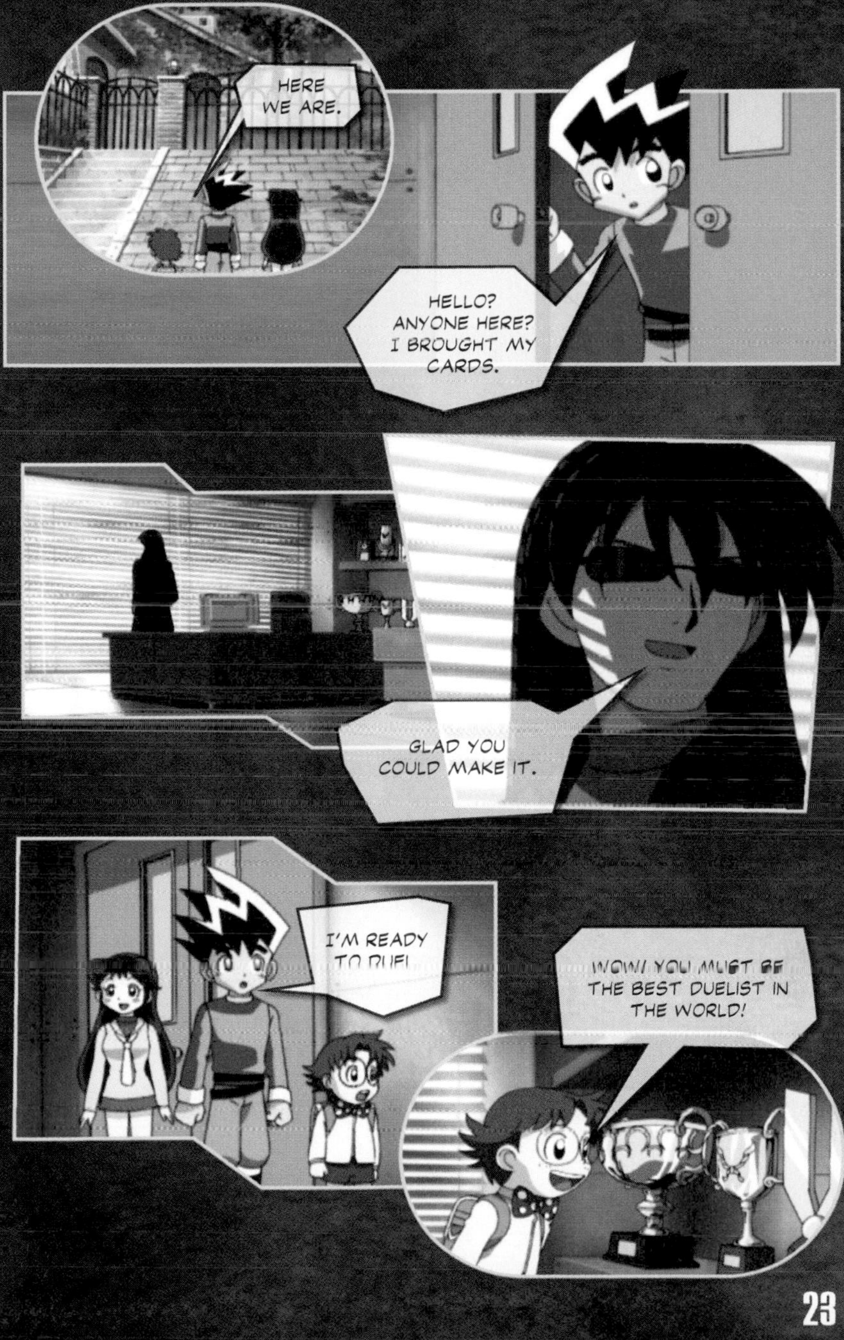
HERE WE ARE.
HELLO? ANYONE HERE? I BROUGHT MY CARDS.
GLAD YOU COULD MAKE IT.
I'M READY TO DUEL!
WOW! YOU MUST BE THE BEST DUELIST IN THE WORLD!

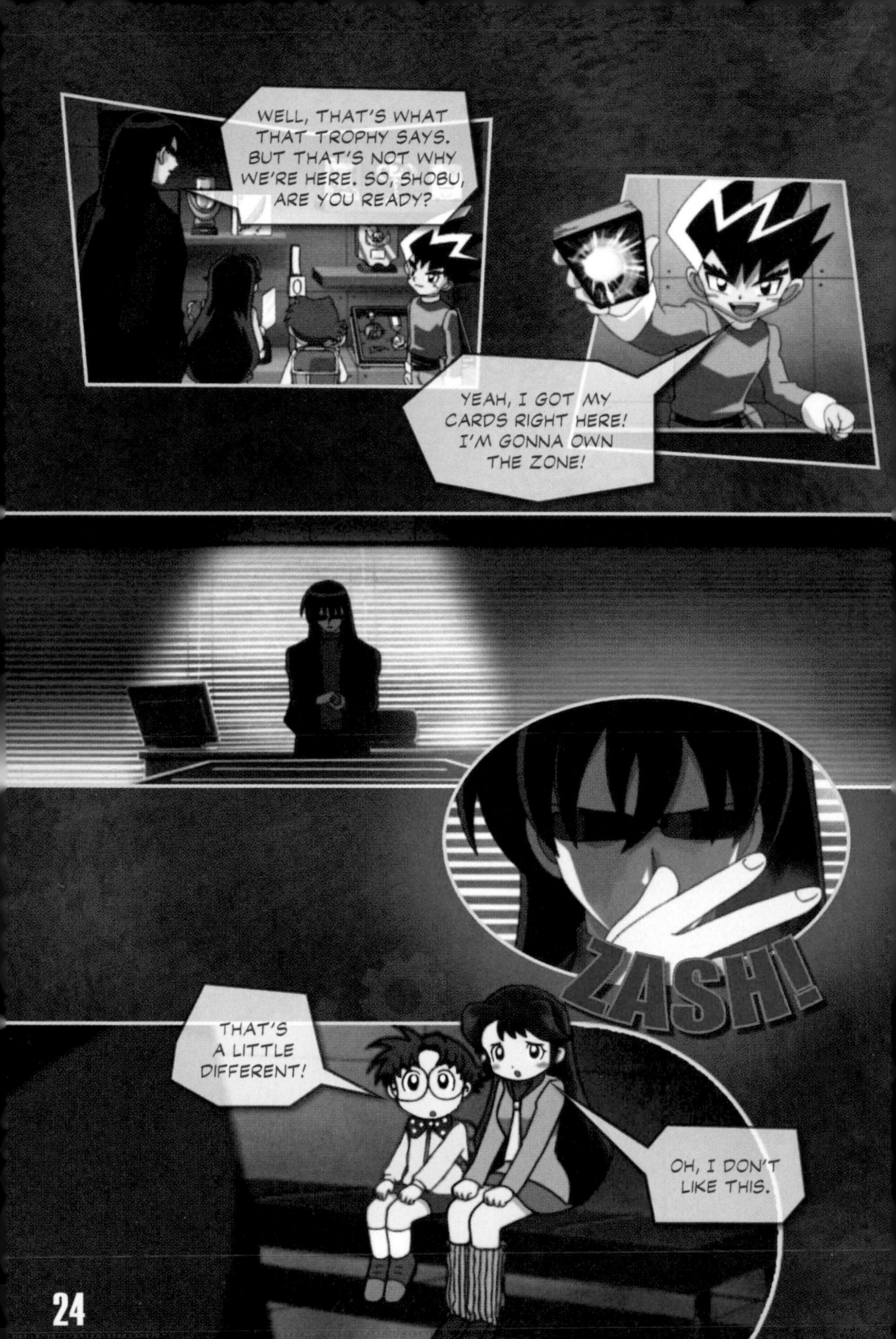
WELL, THAT'S WHAT THAT TROPHY SAYS. BUT THAT'S NOT WHY WE'RE HERE. SO, SHOBU, ARE YOU READY?
YEAH, I GOT MY CARDS RIGHT HERE! I'M GONNA OWN THE ZONE!
ZASH!
THAT'S A LITTLE DIFFERENT!
OH, I DON'T LIKE THIS.

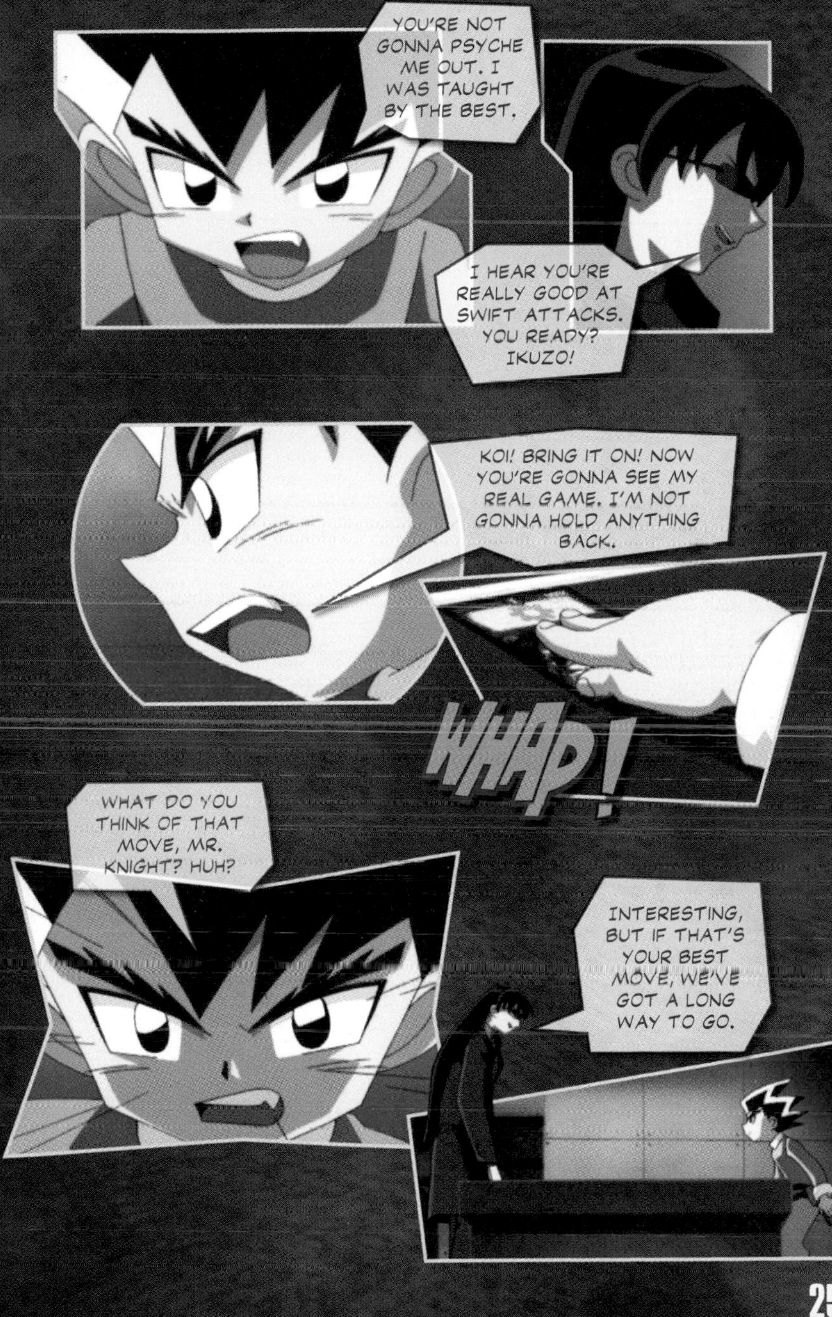
YOU'RE NOT GONNA PSYCHE ME OUT. I WAS TAUGHT BY THE BEST.
I HEAR YOU'RE REALLY GOOD AT SWIFT ATTACKS. YOU READY? IKUZO!
KOI! BRING IT ON! NOW YOU'RE GONNA SEE MY REAL GAME. I'M NOT GONNA HOLD ANYTHING BACK.
WHAP!
WHAT DO YOU THINK OF THAT MOVE, MR. KNIGHT? HUH?
INTERESTING, BUT IF THAT'S YOUR BEST MOVE, WE'VE GOT A LONG WAY TO GO.

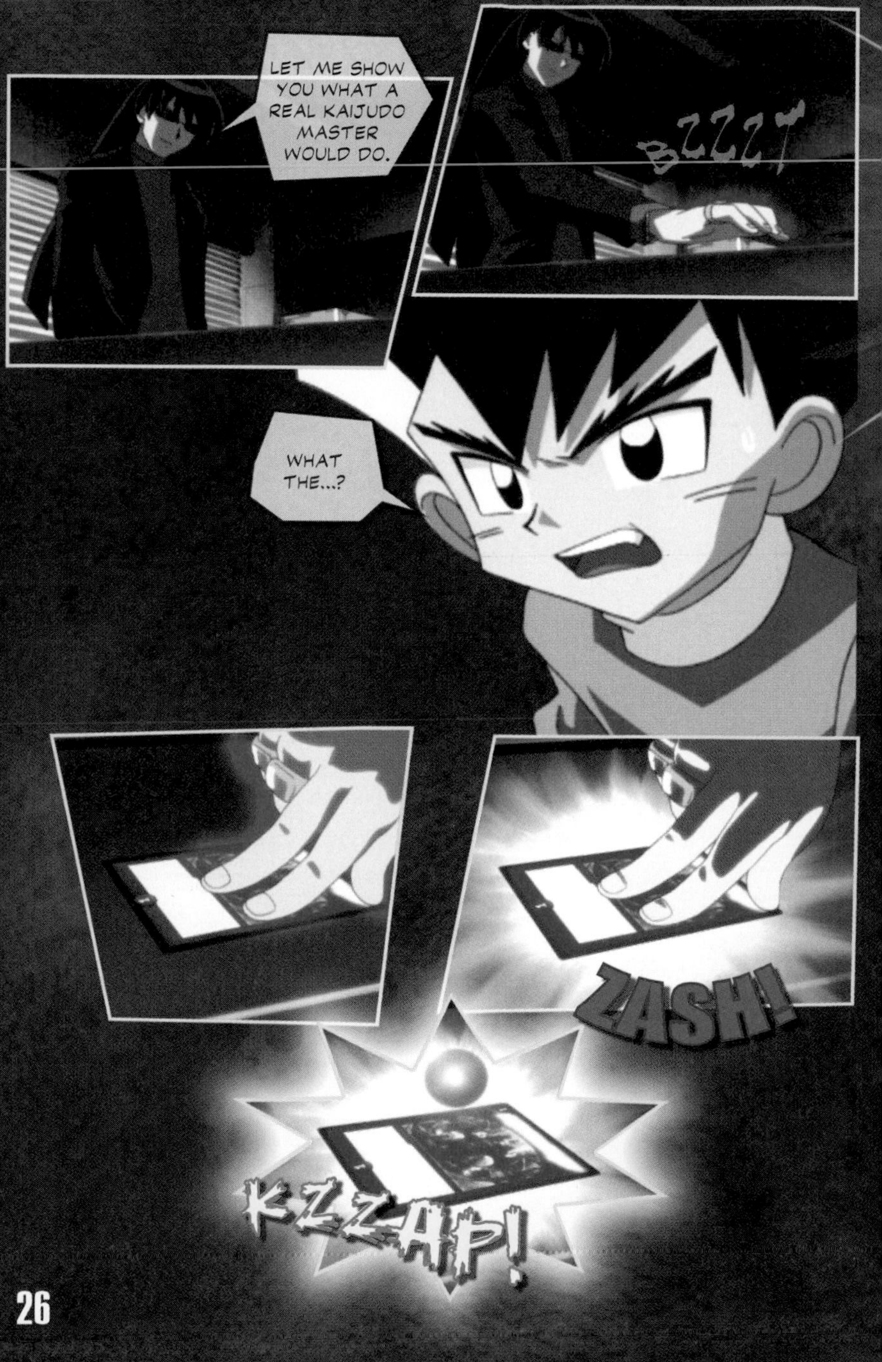
LET ME SHOW YOU WHAT A REAL KAIJUDO MASTER WOULD DO.
BZZZT
WHAT THE...?
ZASH!
KZZAP!

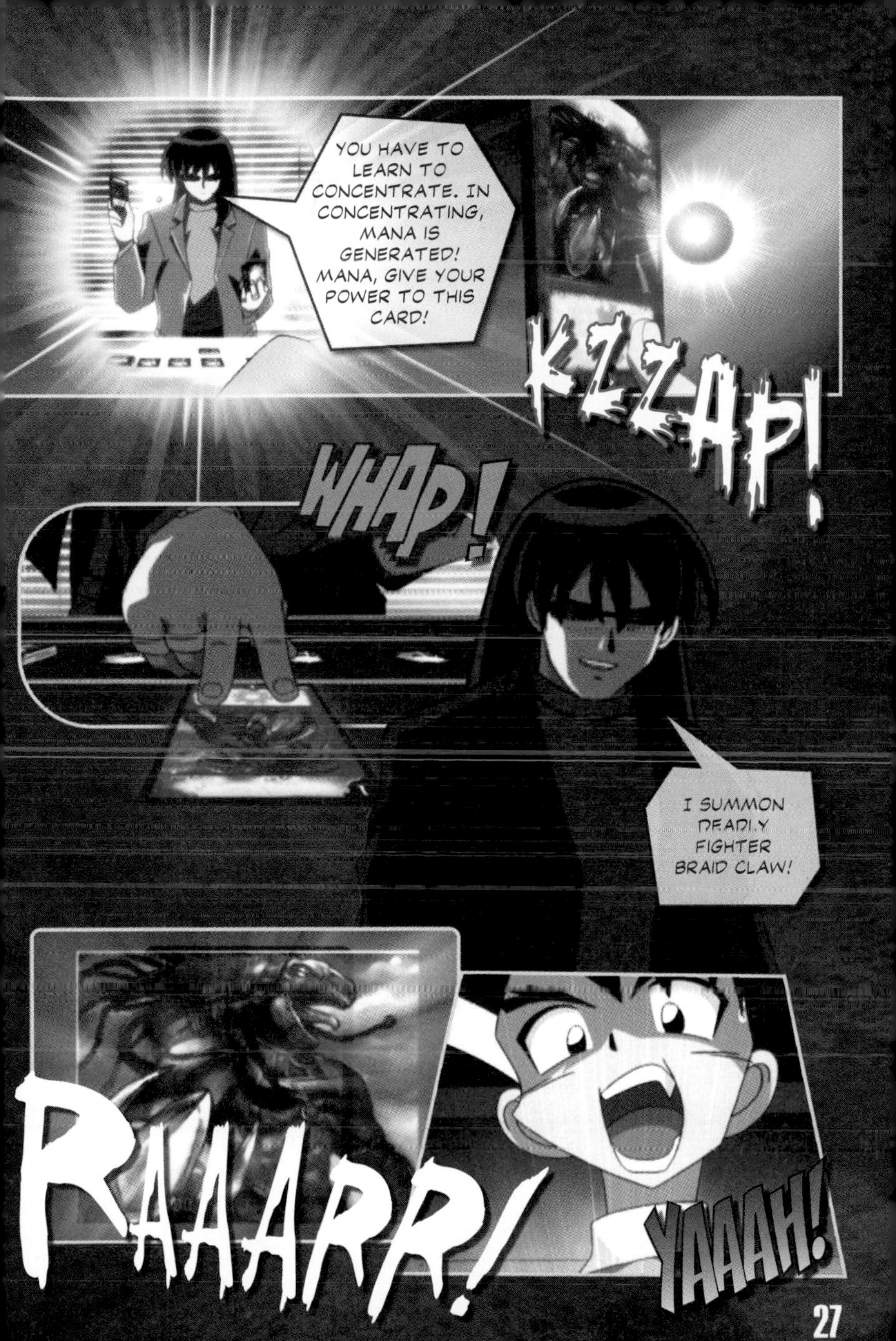
YOU HAVE TO LEARN TO CONCENTRATE. IN CONCENTRATING, MANA IS GENERATED! MANA, GIVE YOUR POWER TO THIS CARD!
KZZAP!
WHAP!
I SUMMON DEADLY FIGHTER BRAID CLAW!
RAAARR!
YAAAH!

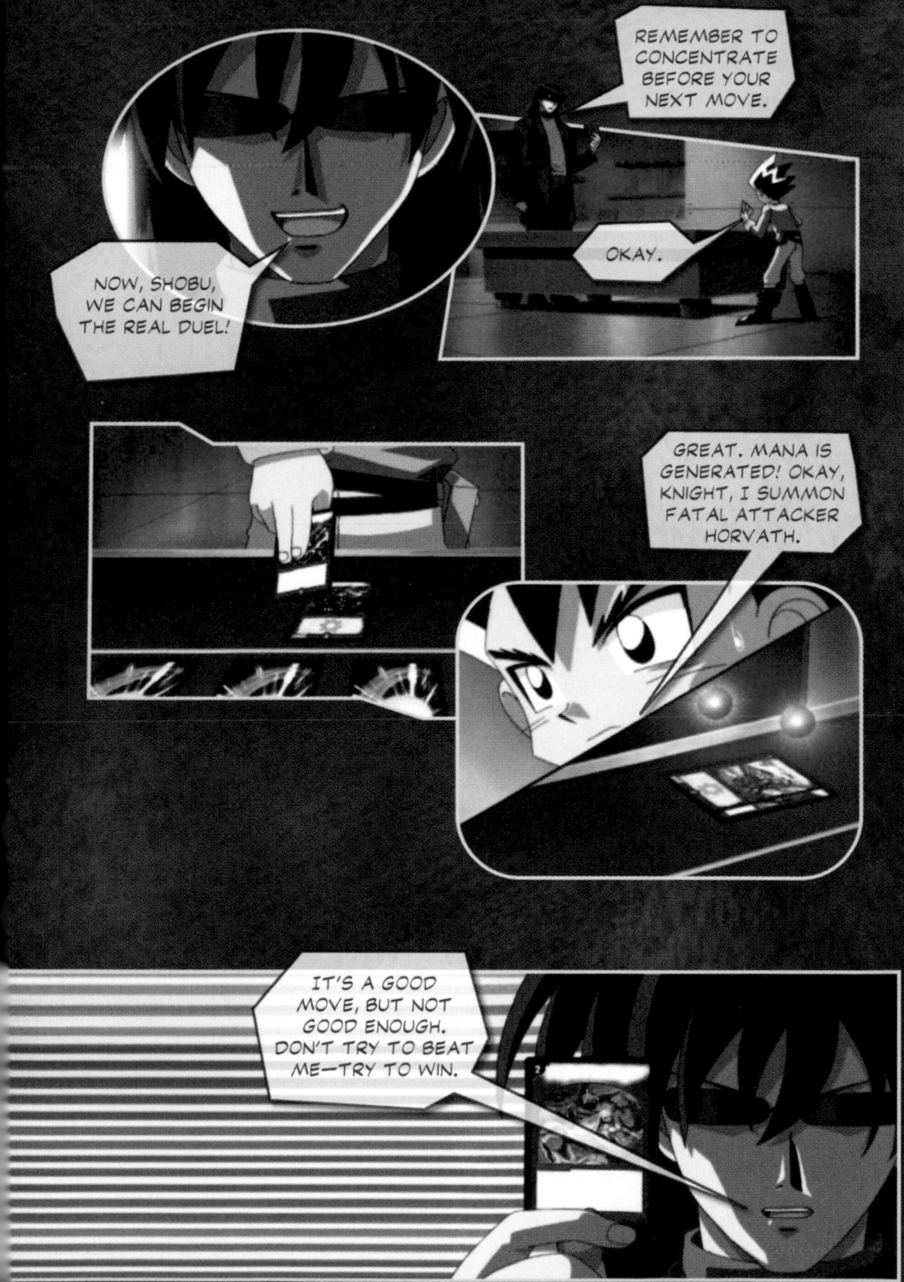
REMEMBER TO CONCENTRATE BEFORE YOUR NEXT MOVE.
NOW, SHOBU, WE CAN BEGIN THE REAL DUEL!
OKAY.
GREAT. MANA IS GENERATED! OKAY, KNIGHT, I SUMMON FATAL ATTACKER HORVATH.
IT'S A GOOD MOVE, BUT NOT GOOD ENOUGH. DON'T TRY TO BEAT ME—TRY TO WIN.

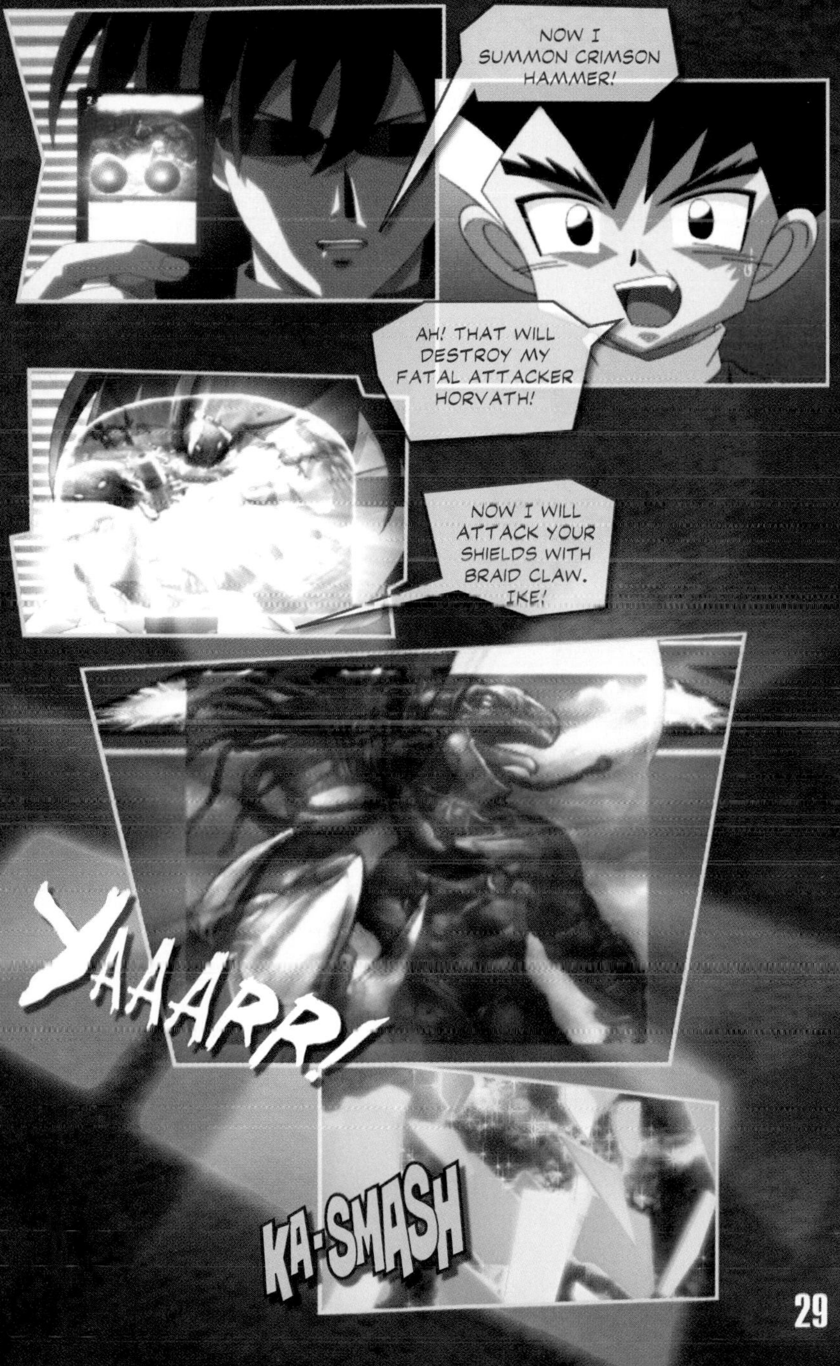
NOW I SUMMON CRIMSON HAMMER!
AH! THAT WILL DESTROY MY FATAL ATTACKER HORVATH!
NOW I WILL ATTACK YOUR SHIELDS WITH BRAID CLAW. IKE!
YAAARR!
KA-SMASH

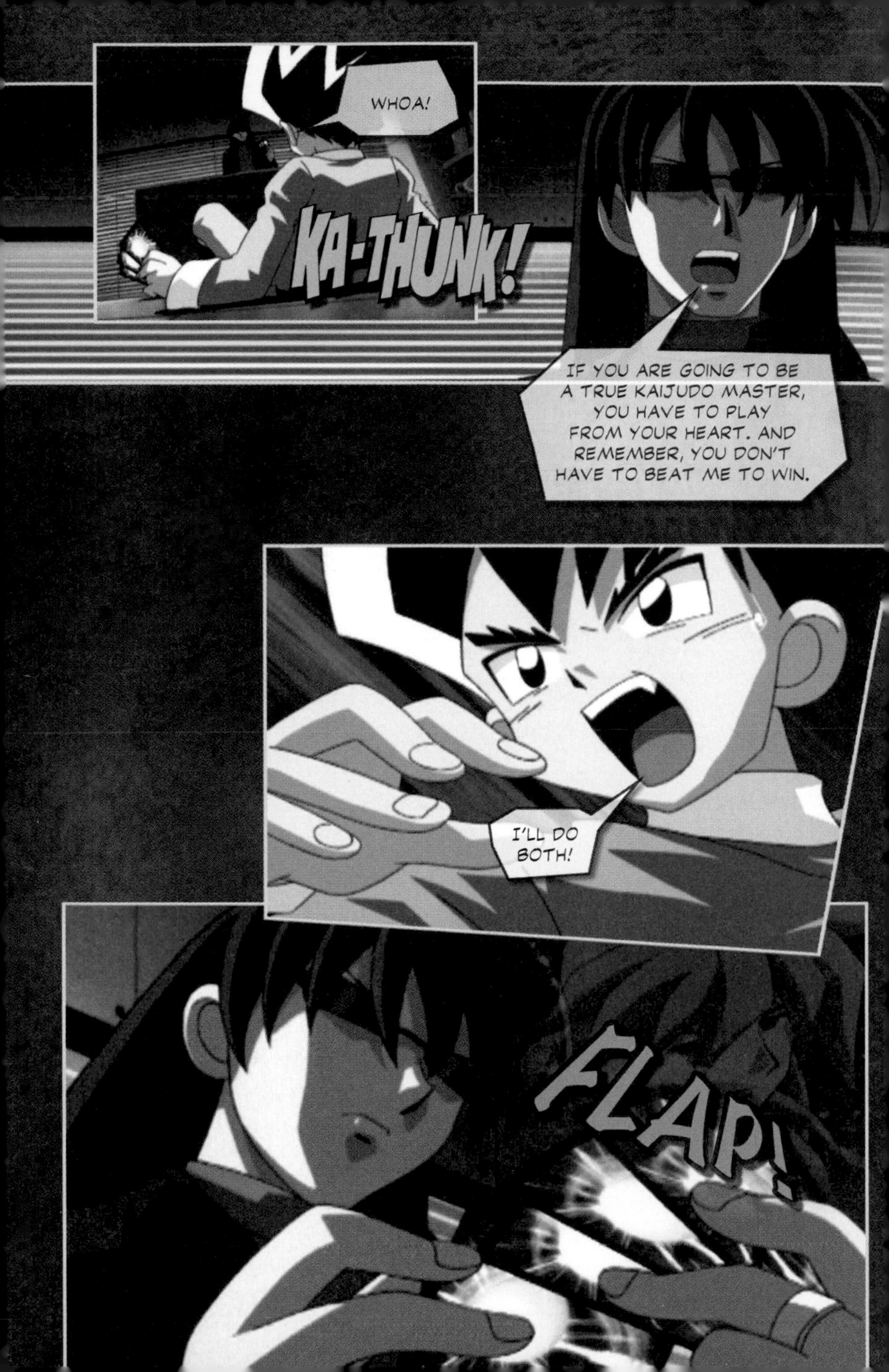
WHOA!
KA-THUNK!
IF YOU ARE GOING TO BE A TRUE KAIJUDO MASTER, YOU HAVE TO PLAY FROM YOUR HEART. AND REMEMBER, YOU DON'T HAVE TO BEAT ME TO WIN.
I'LL DO BOTH!
FLAP!

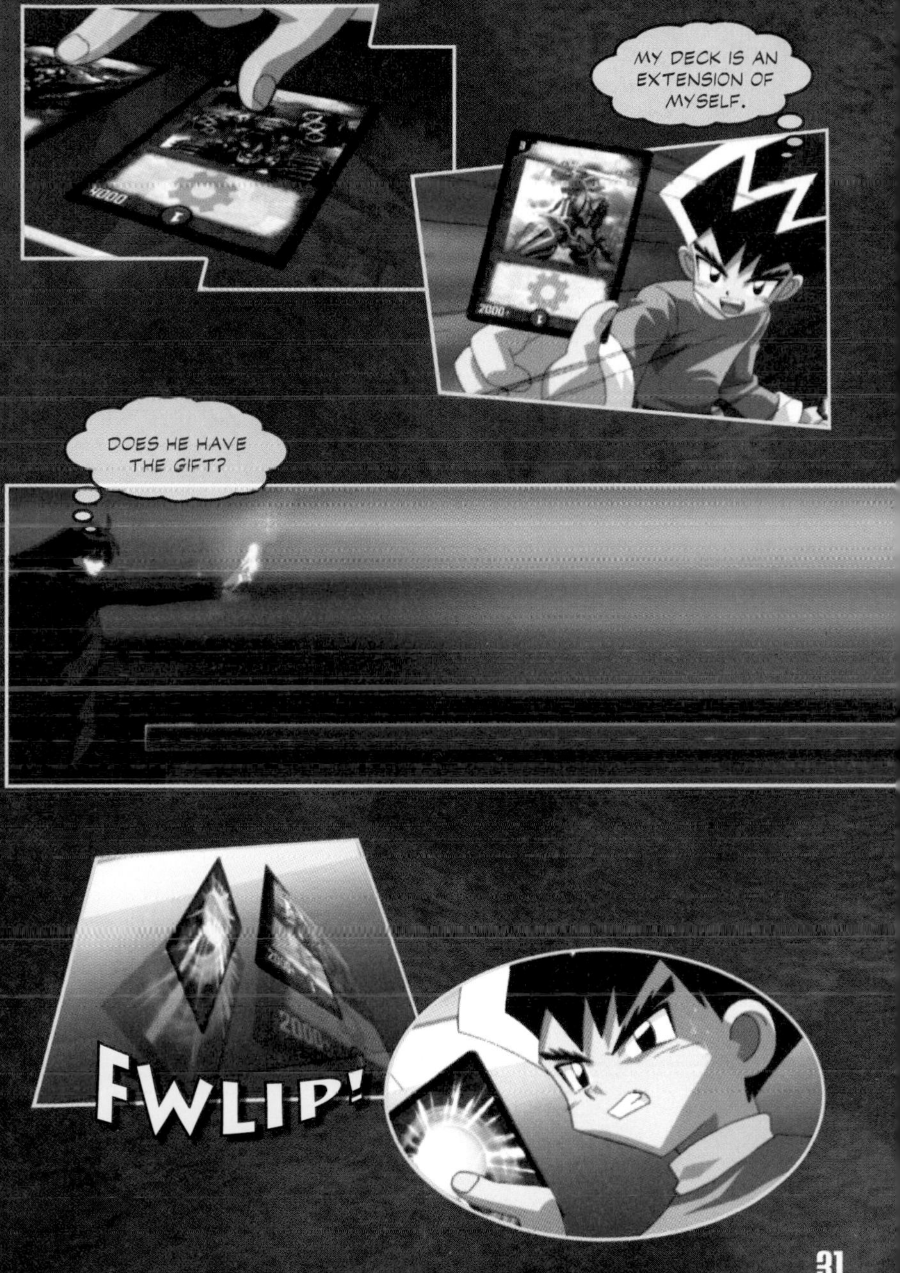
MY DECK IS AN EXTENSION OF MYSELF.
DOES HE HAVE THE GIFT?
FWLIP!

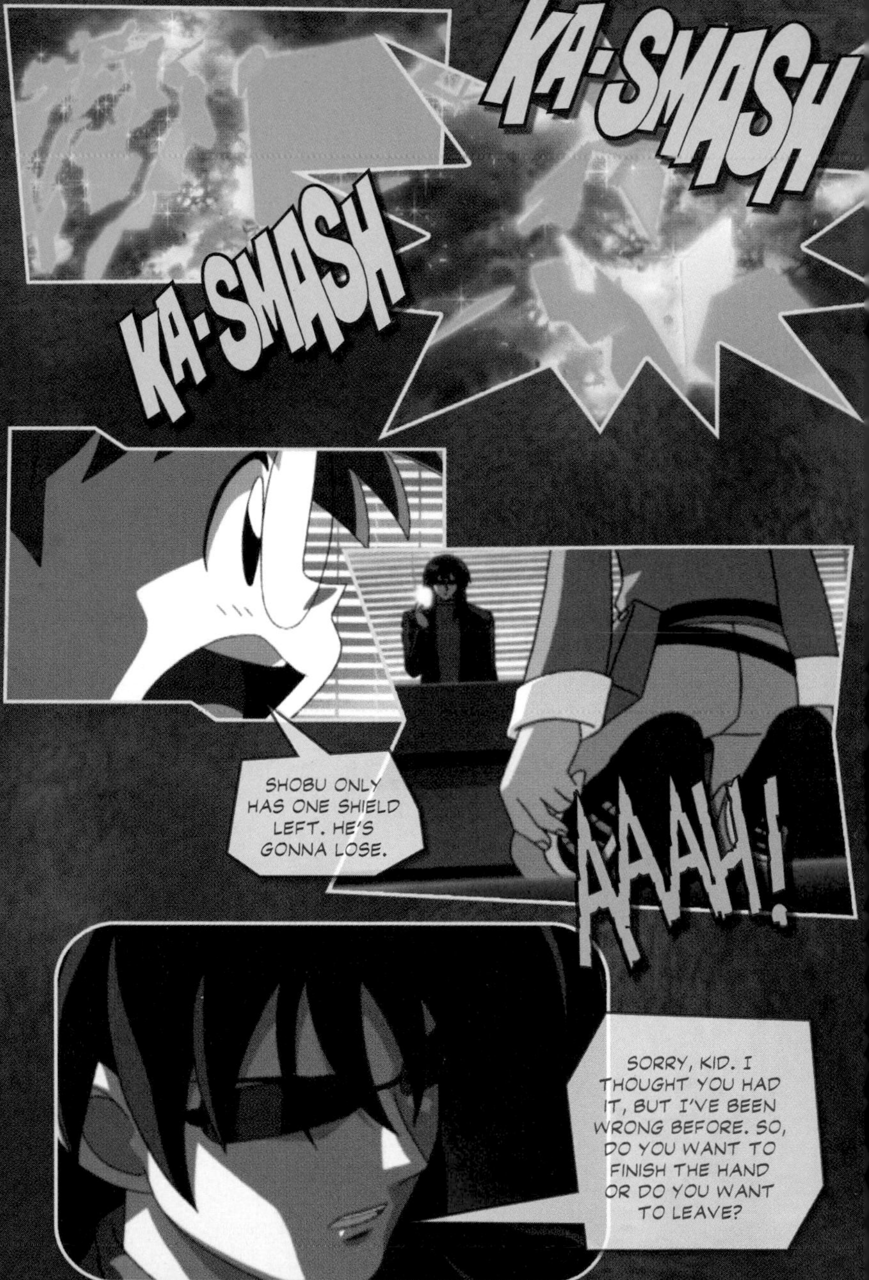
KA-SMASH
KA-SMASH
SHOBU ONLY HAS ONE SHIELD LEFT. HE'S GONNA LOSE.
AAAH!
SORRY, KID. I THOUGHT YOU HAD IT, BUT I'VE BEEN WRONG BEFORE. SO, DO YOU WANT TO FINISH THE HAND OR DO YOU WANT TO LEAVE?

I DON'T BELIEVE THIS. I ONLY HAVE ONE SHIELD LEFT. I DON'T HAVE THE RIGHT CARDS. I CAN'T POSSIBLY WIN.

IT'S OKAY, SHOBU, YOU PLAYED A GOOD ONE!

YEAH, YOU REALLY OWNED THE ZONE!

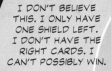

I DIDN'T OWN ANYTHING.

NOW YOU'RE STARTING TO SOUND LIKE A KAIJUDO MASTER!

WHAT?

BUT SOUNDING LIKE ONE AND BEING ONE ARE STILL TWO DIFFERENT THINGS. IF YOU CONTINUE TO PLAY ME, I'M PROBABLY GOING TO BEAT YOU.

BUT I CAN BEAT YOU AND YOU CAN STILL WIN. THAT'S WHAT "OWNING THE ZONE" IS. IF YOU CAN'T UNDERSTAND THIS CONCEPT, YOU SHOULD QUIT.

I QUIT.

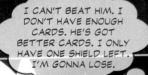

I CAN'T BEAT HIM. I DON'T HAVE ENOUGH CARDS. HE'S GOT BETTER CARDS. I ONLY HAVE ONE SHIELD LEFT. I'M GONNA LOSE.

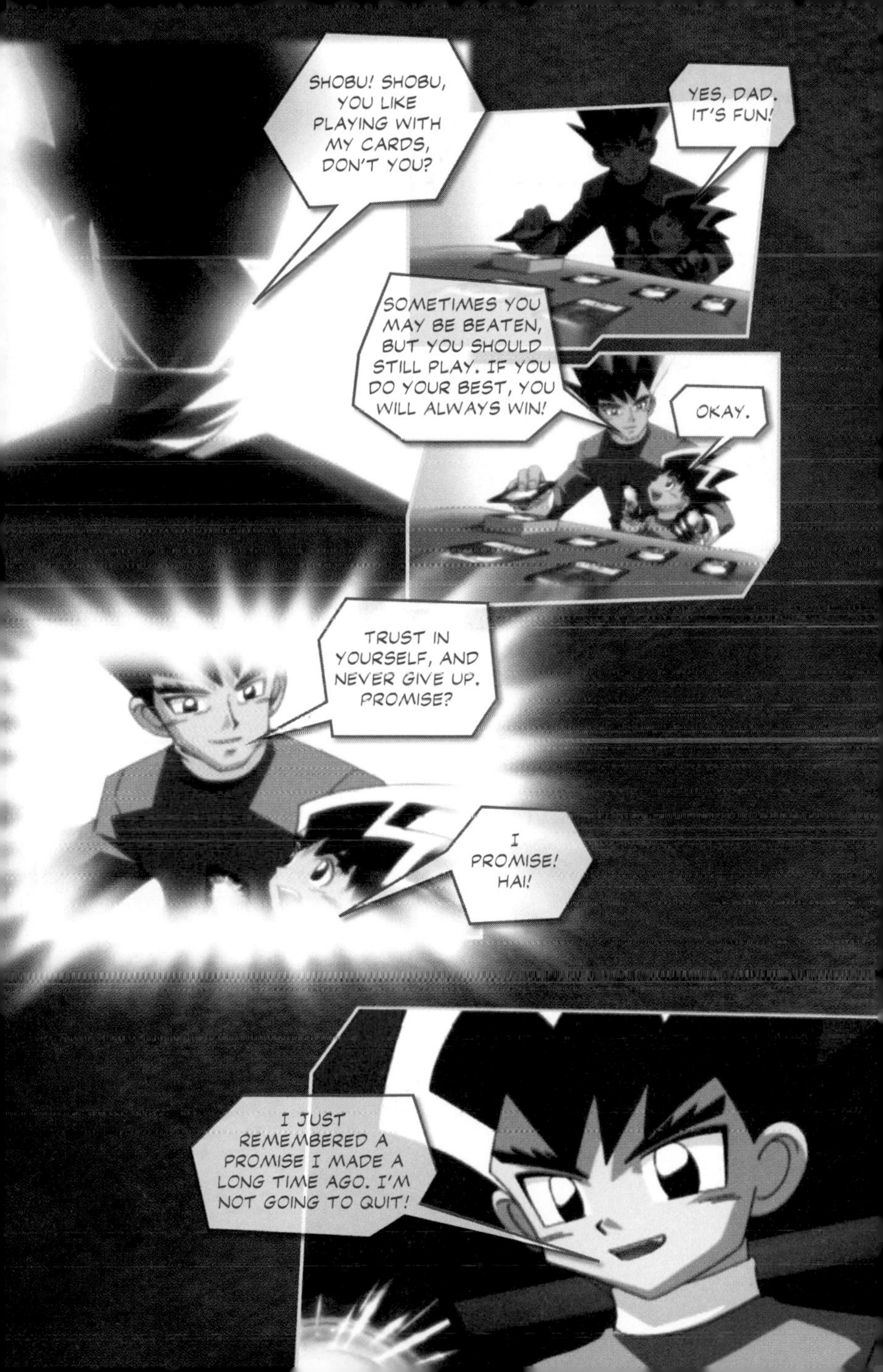
SHOBU! SHOBU, YOU LIKE PLAYING WITH MY CARDS, DON'T YOU?
YES, DAD. IT'S FUN!
SOMETIMES YOU MAY BE BEATEN, BUT YOU SHOULD STILL PLAY. IF YOU DO YOUR BEST, YOU WILL ALWAYS WIN!
OKAY.
TRUST IN YOURSELF, AND NEVER GIVE UP. PROMISE?
I PROMISE! HAI!
I JUST REMEMBERED A PROMISE I MADE A LONG TIME AGO. I'M NOT GOING TO QUIT!

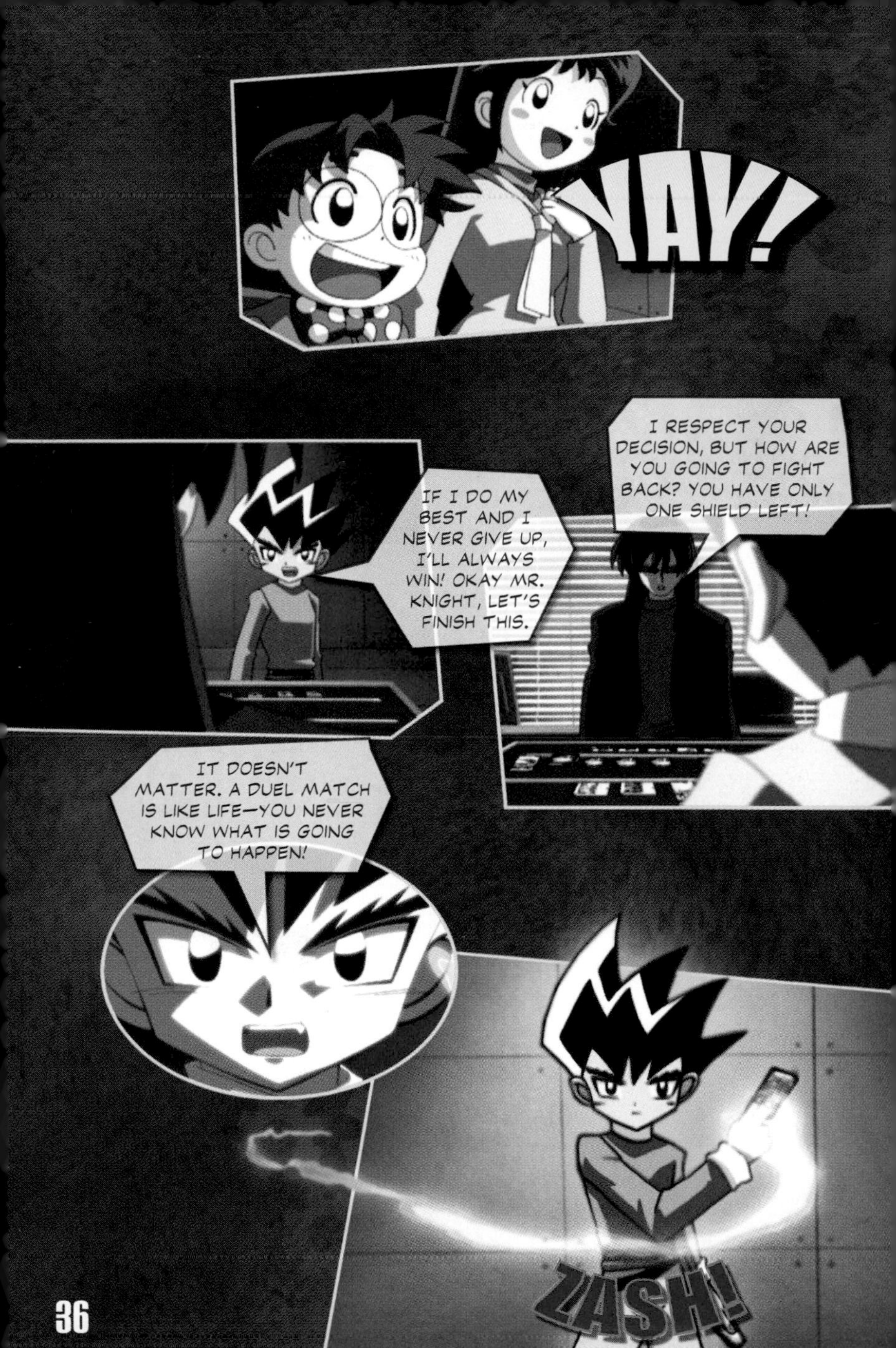
YAY!
IF I DO MY BEST AND I NEVER GIVE UP, I'LL ALWAYS WIN! OKAY MR. KNIGHT, LET'S FINISH THIS.
I RESPECT YOUR DECISION, BUT HOW ARE YOU GOING TO FIGHT BACK? YOU HAVE ONLY ONE SHIELD LEFT!
IT DOESN'T MATTER. A DUEL MATCH IS LIKE LIFE—YOU NEVER KNOW WHAT IS GOING TO HAPPEN!
ZASH!

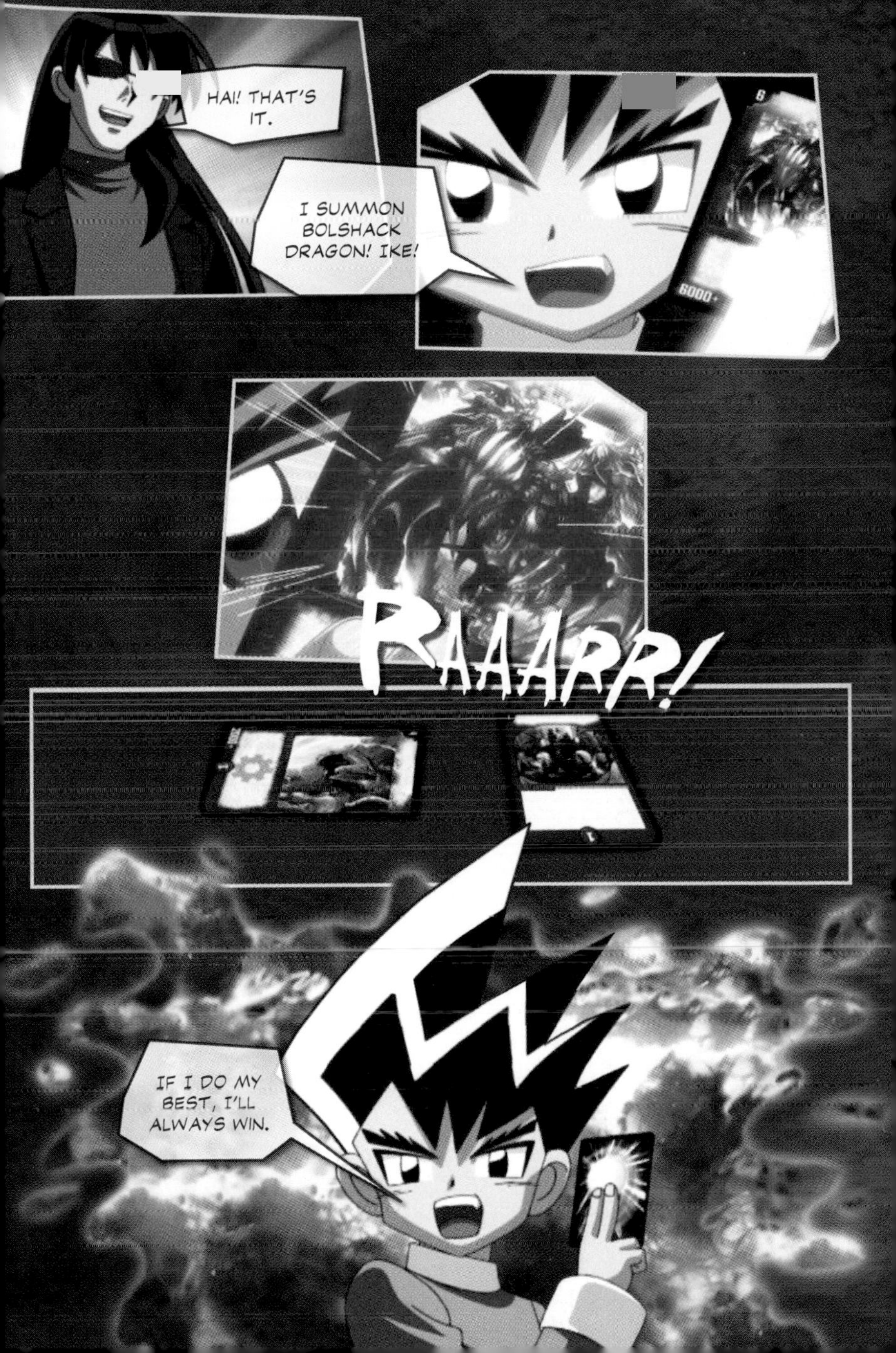
HAI! THAT'S IT.
I SUMMON BOLSHACK DRAGON! IKE!
6000+
RAAARR!
IF I DO MY BEST, I'LL ALWAYS WIN.

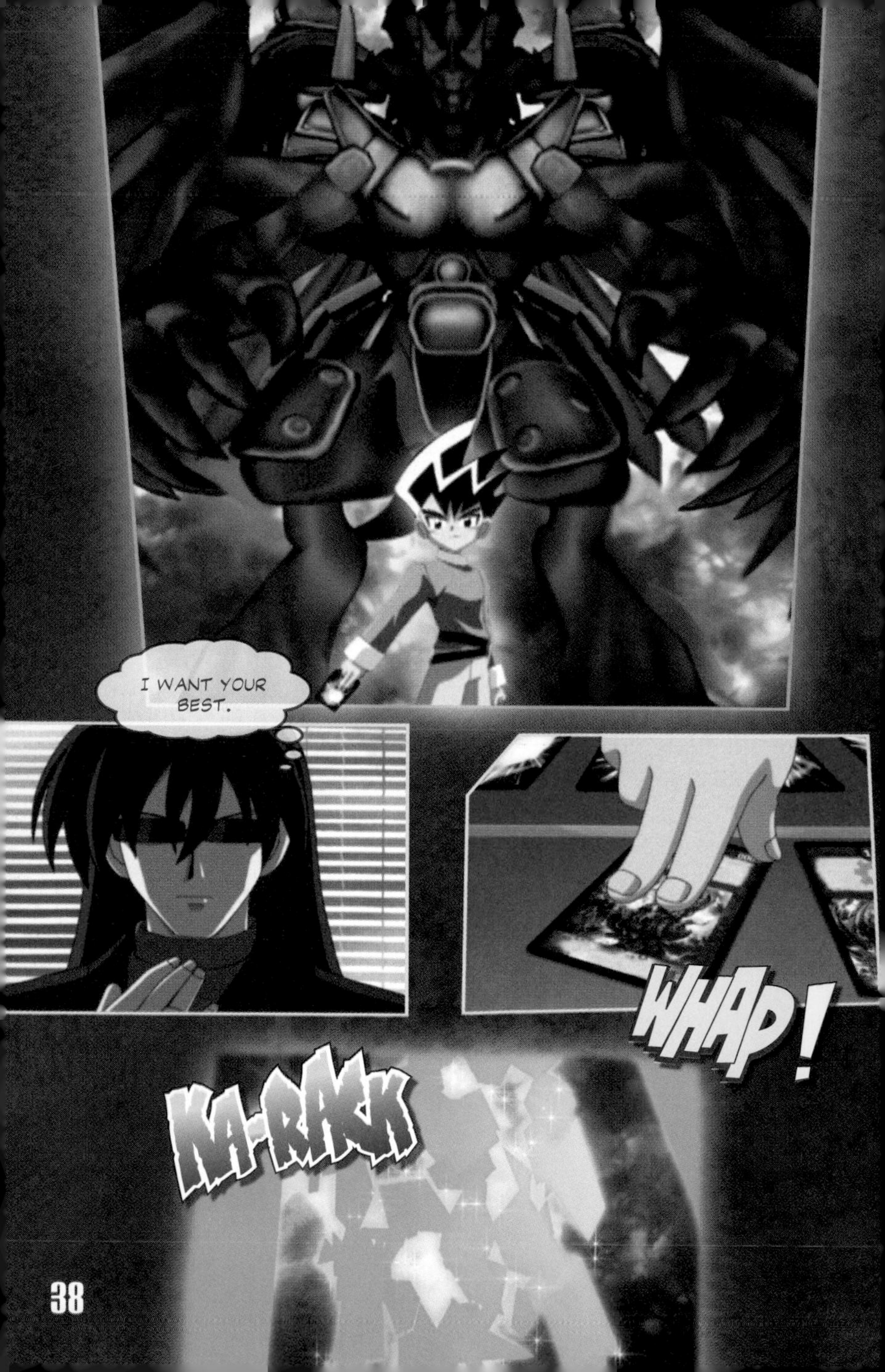
I WANT YOUR BEST.
WHAP!
KA-RACK

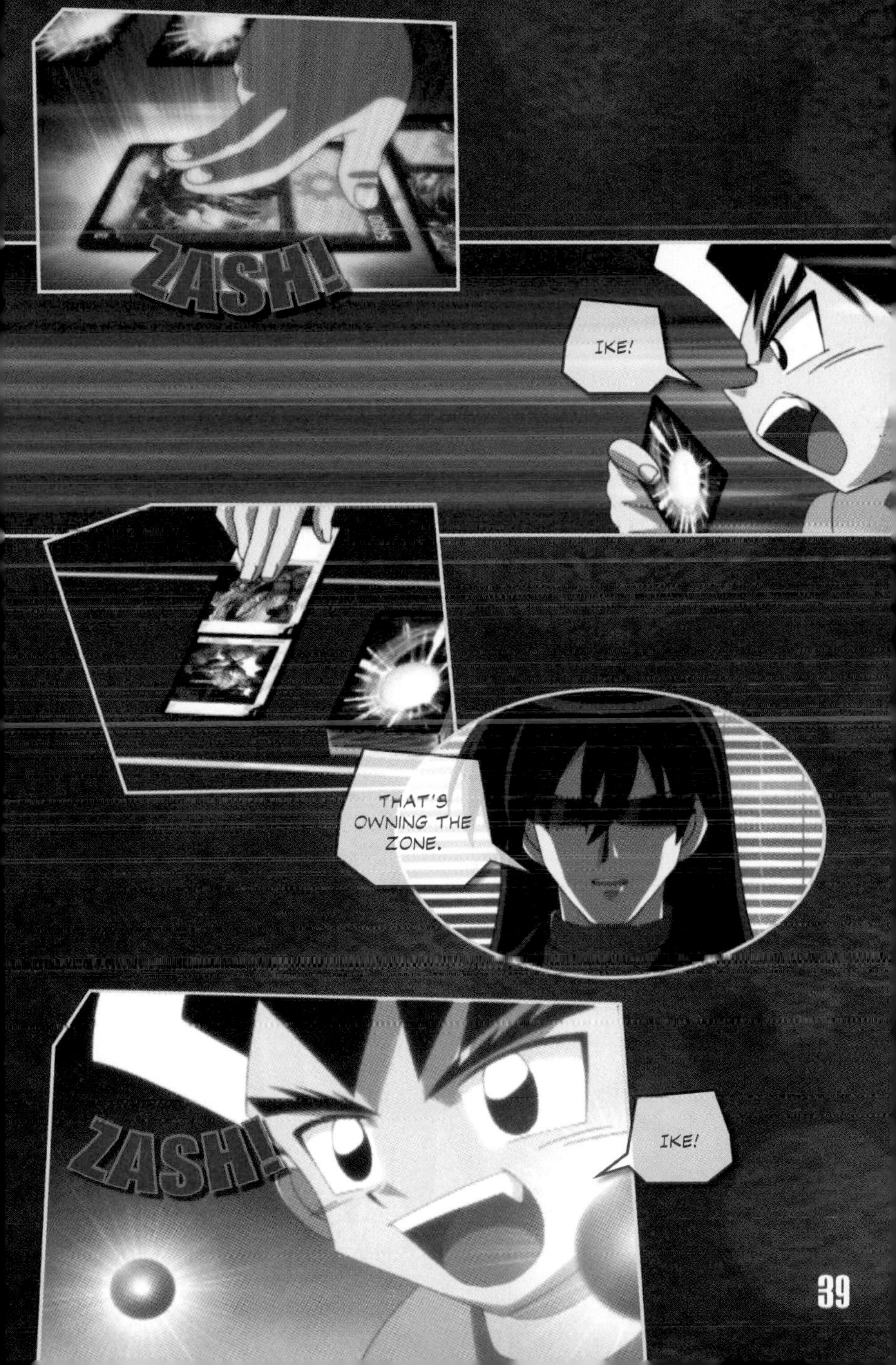
ZASH!
IKE!
THAT'S OWNING THE ZONE.
ZASH!
IKE!

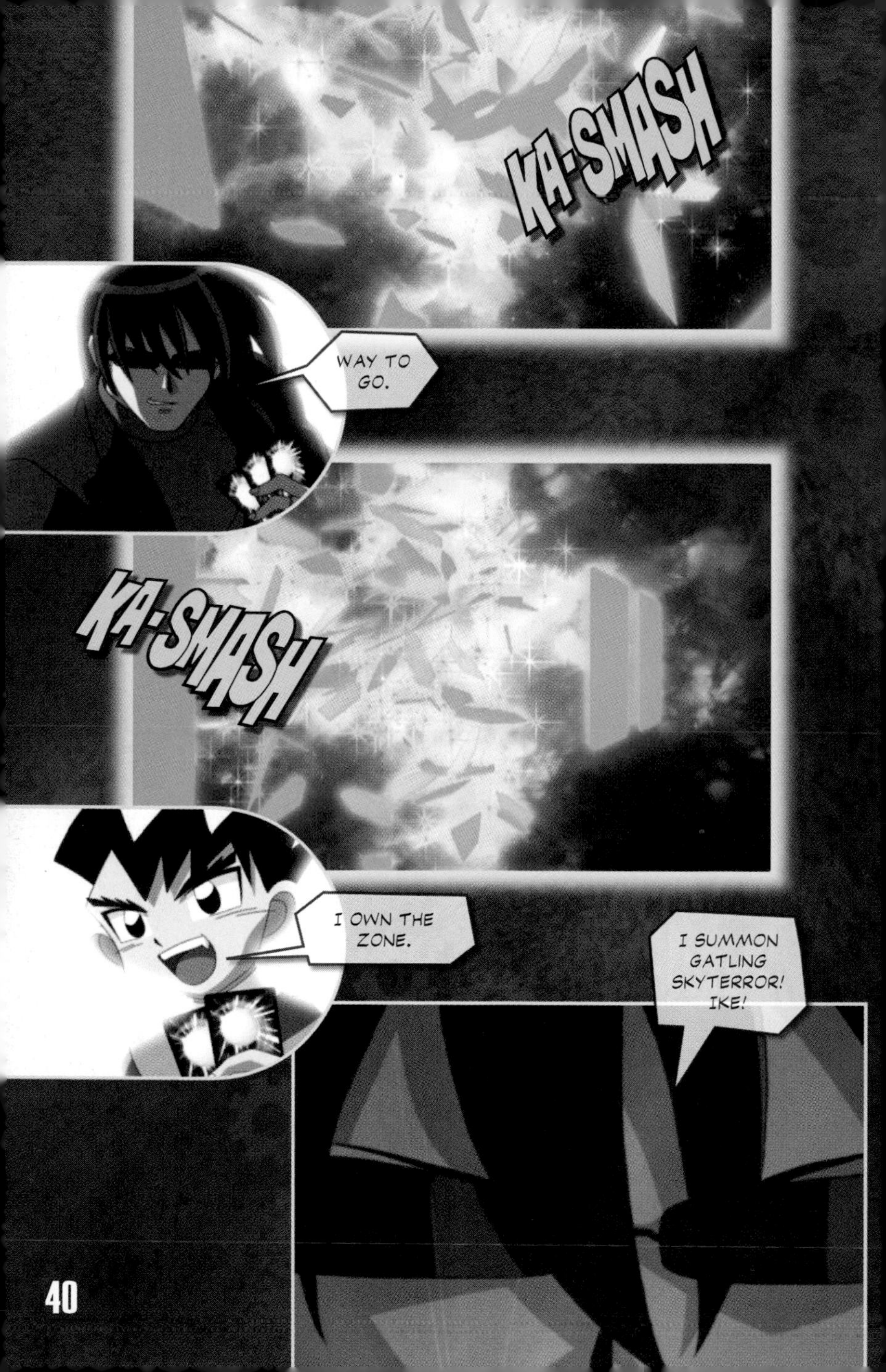
KA-SMASH
WAY TO GO.
KA-SMASH
I OWN THE ZONE.
I SUMMON GATLING SKYTERROR! IKE!

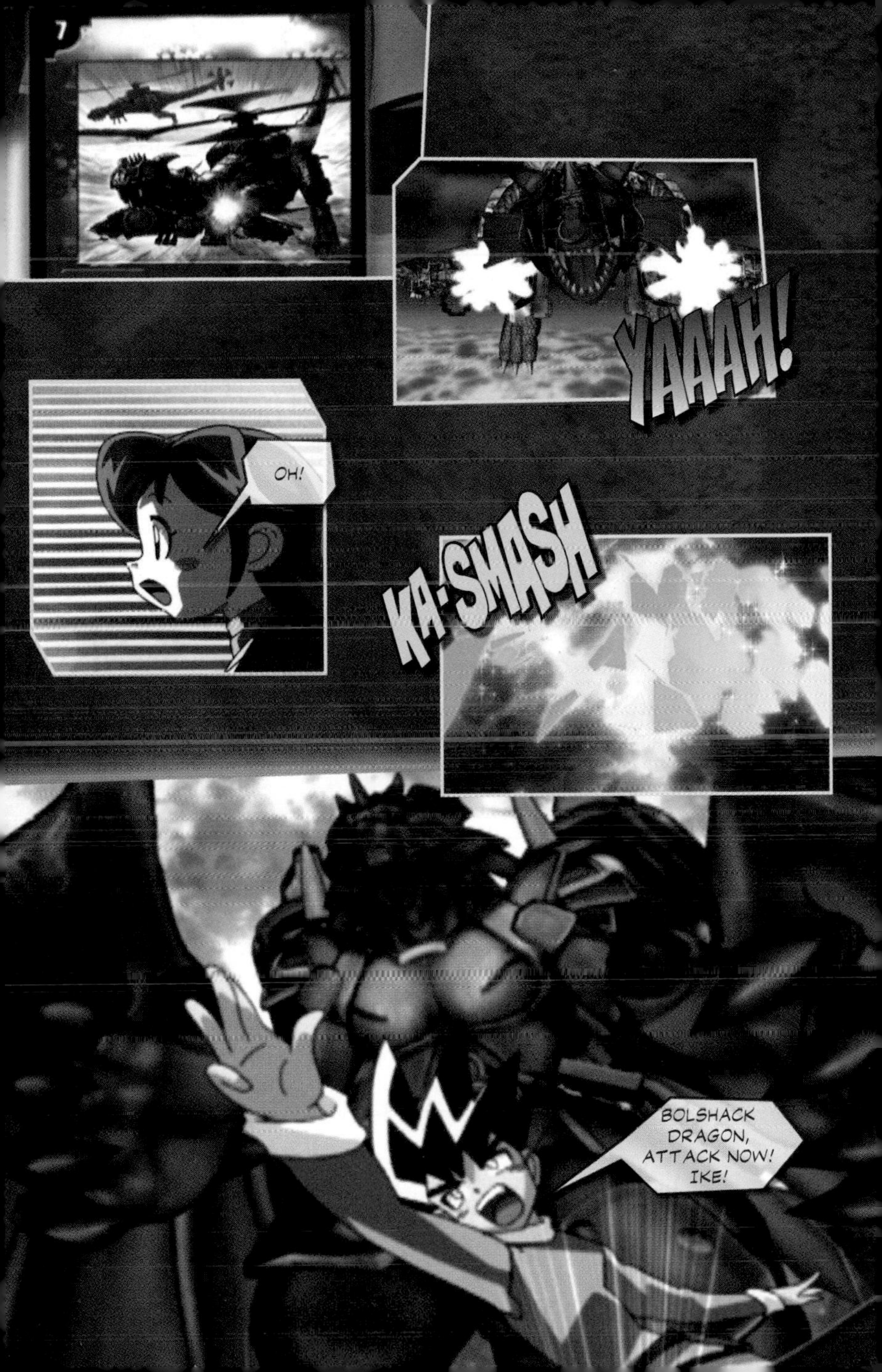
YAAAH!
OH!
KA-SMASH
BOLSHACK DRAGON, ATTACK NOW! IKE!

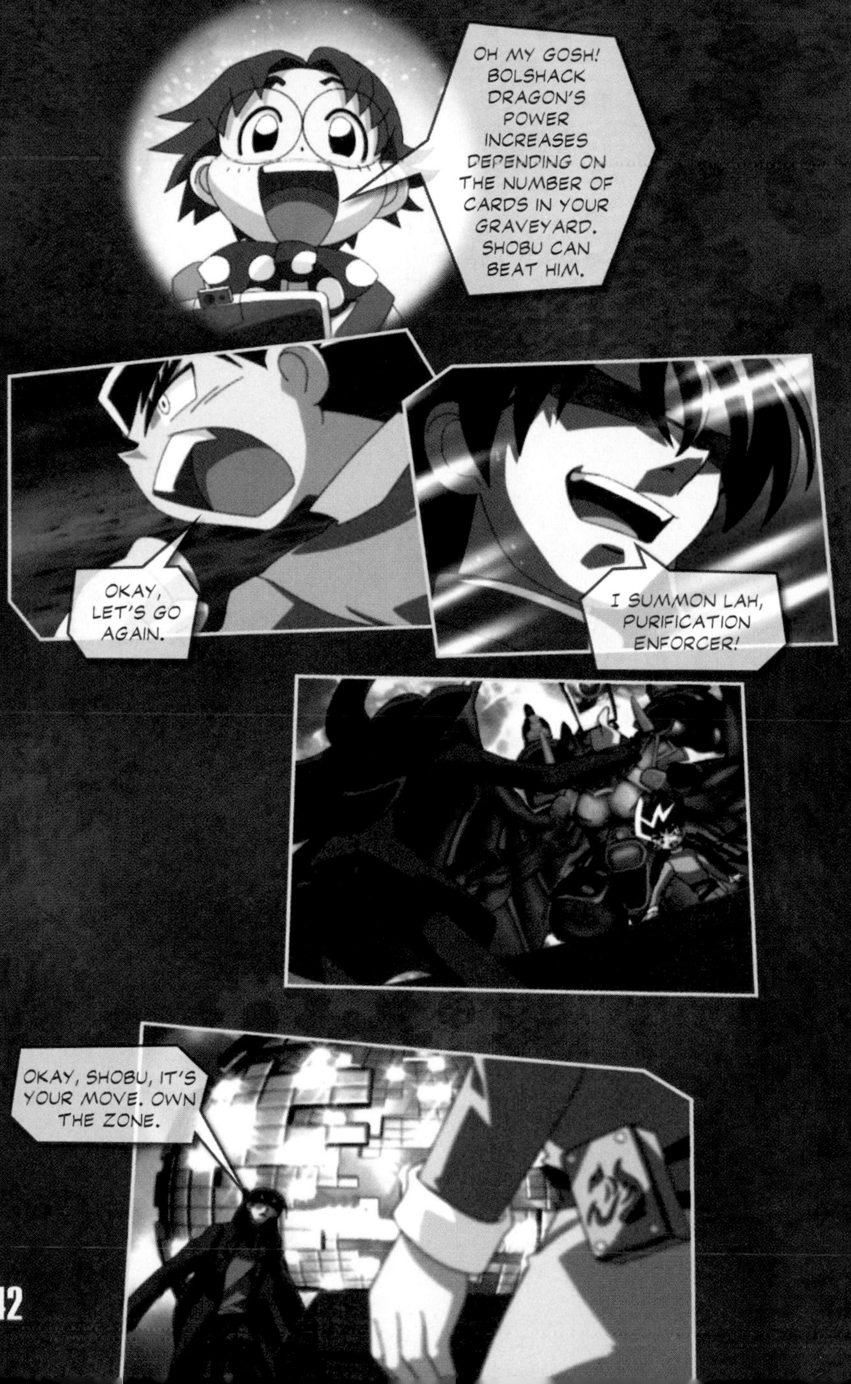
OH MY GOSH! BOLSHACK DRAGON'S POWER INCREASES DEPENDING ON THE NUMBER OF CARDS IN YOUR GRAVEYARD. SHOBU CAN BEAT HIM.
OKAY, LET'S GO AGAIN.
I SUMMON LAH, PURIFICATION ENFORCER!
OKAY, SHOBU, IT'S YOUR MOVE. OWN THE ZONE.

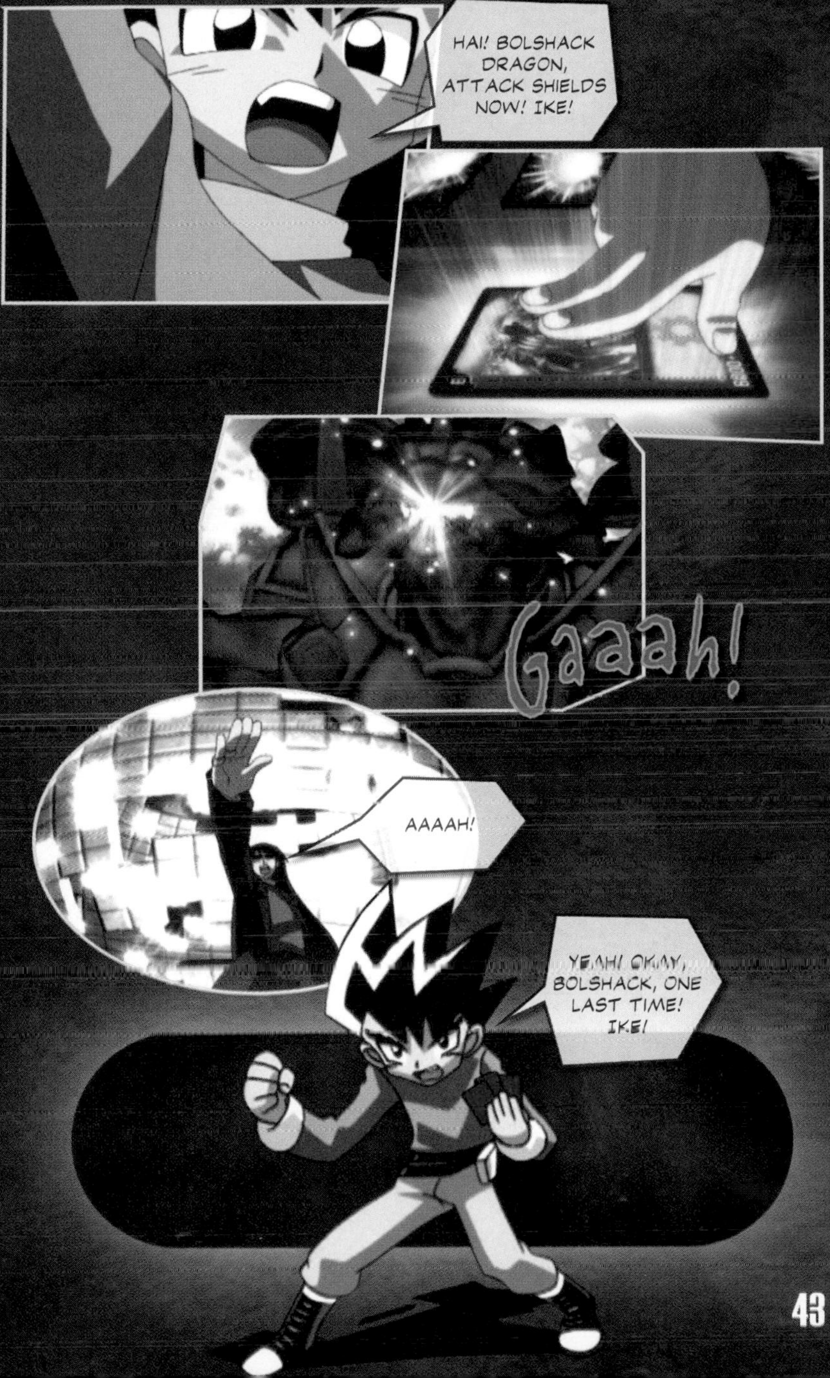
HAI! BOLSHACK DRAGON, ATTACK SHIELDS NOW! IKE!
Gaaah!
AAAAH!
YEAH! OKAY, BOLSHACK, ONE LAST TIME! IKE!

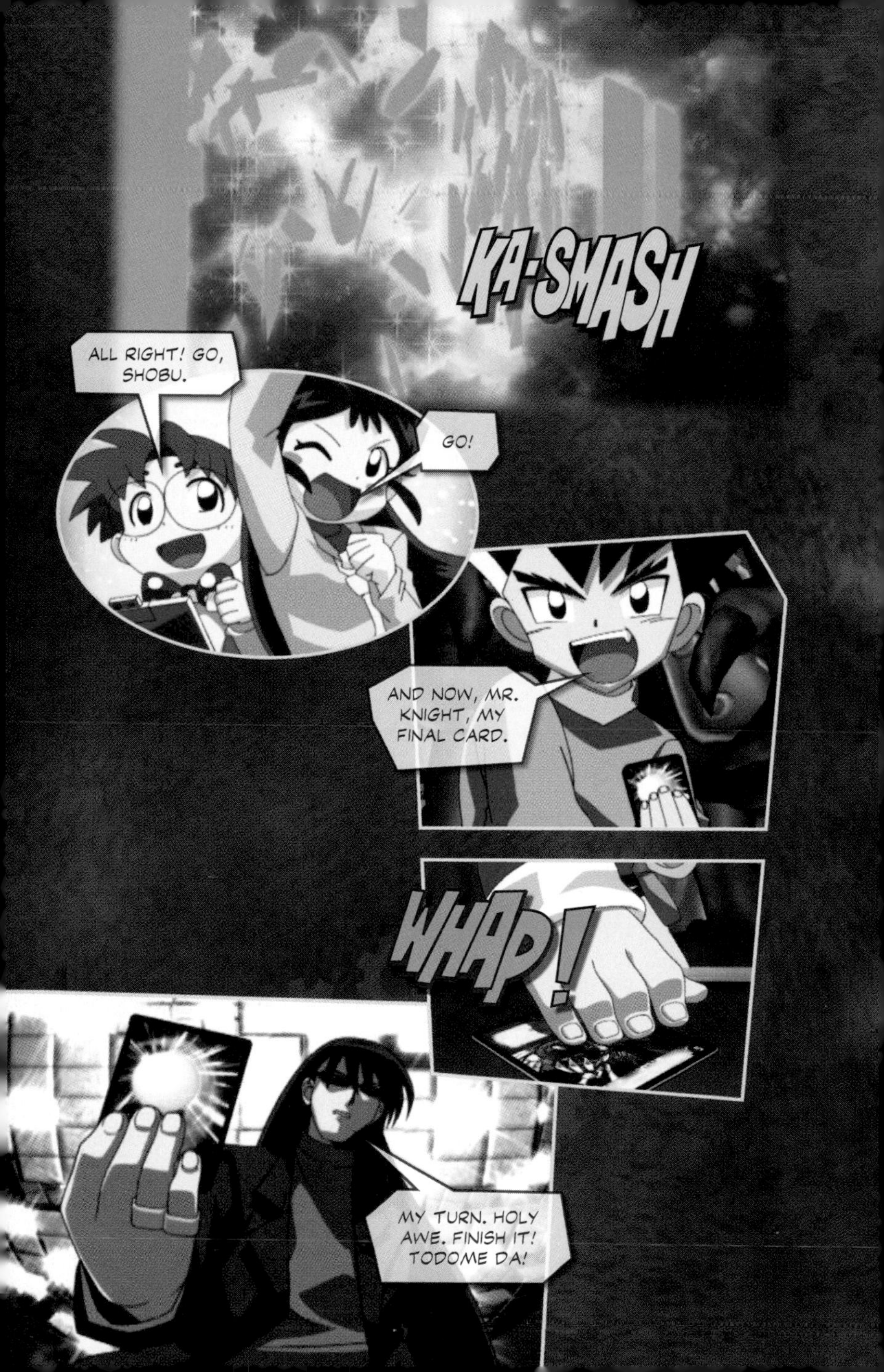
KA-SMASH
ALL RIGHT! GO, SHOBU.
GO!
AND NOW, MR. KNIGHT, MY FINAL CARD.
WHAP!
MY TURN. HOLY AWE. FINISH IT! TODOME DA!

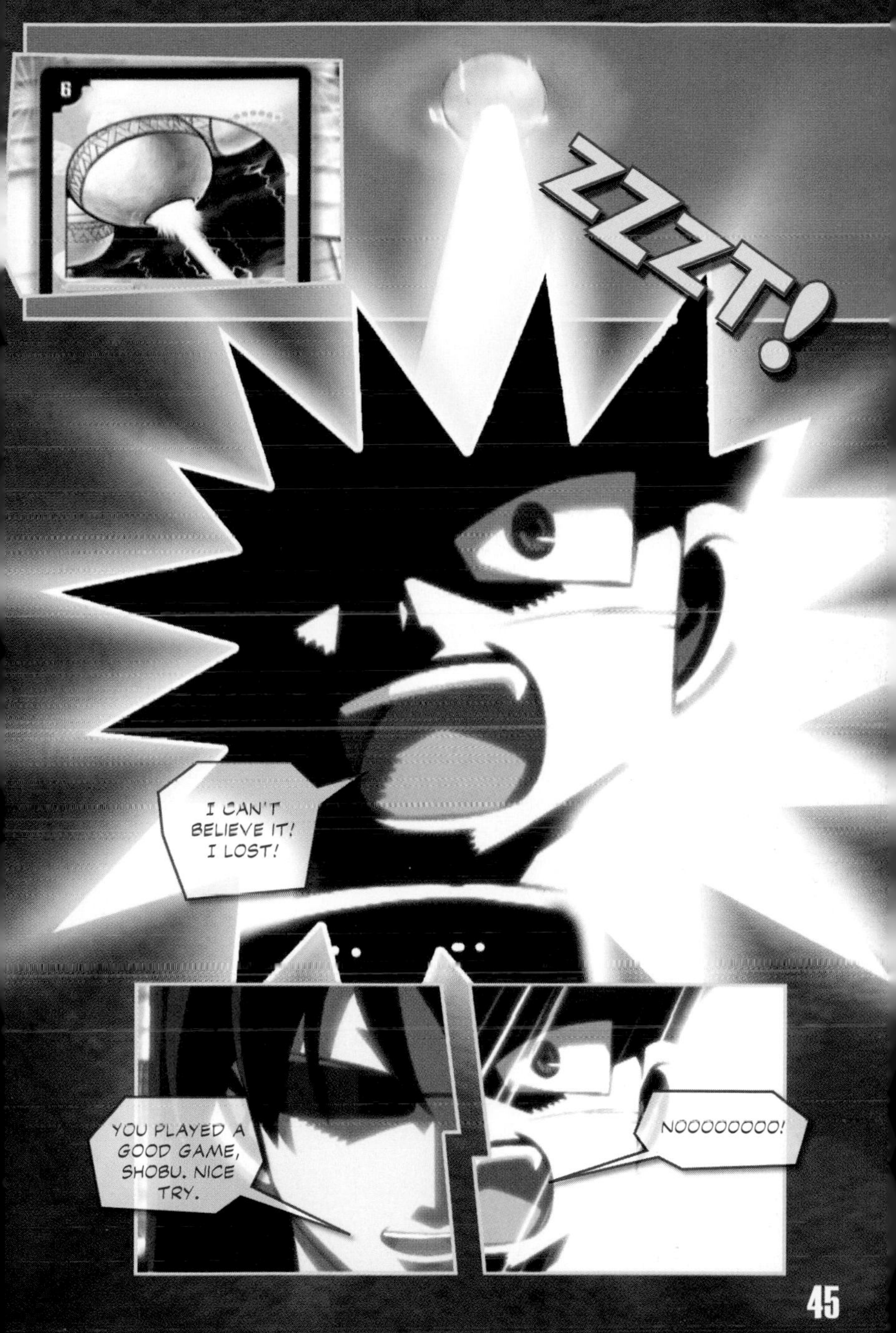
6
ZZZZT!
I CAN'T BELIEVE IT! I LOST!
YOU PLAYED A GOOD GAME, SHOBU. NICE TRY.
NOOOOOOOO!

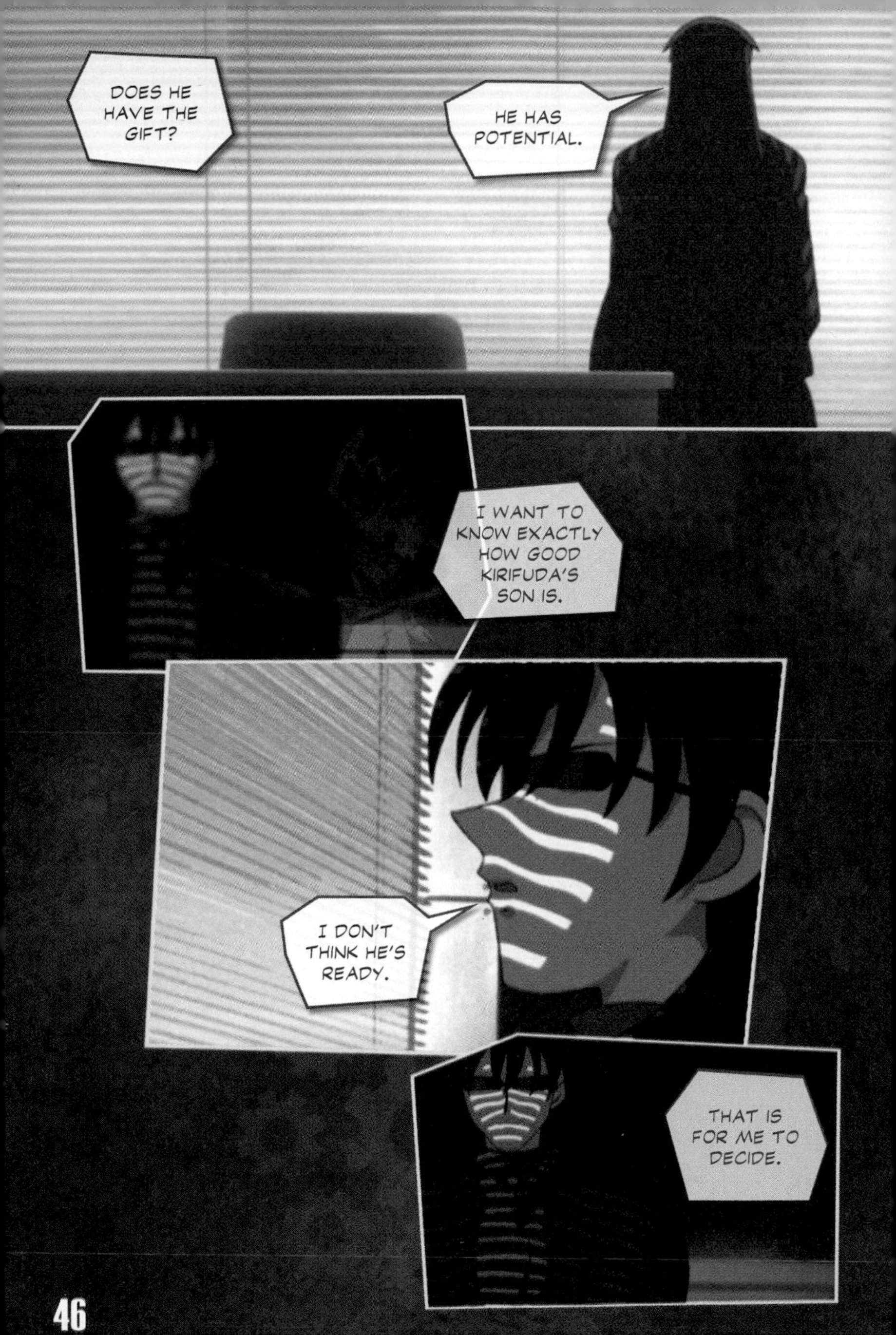
DOES HE HAVE THE GIFT?
HE HAS POTENTIAL.
I WANT TO KNOW EXACTLY HOW GOOD KIRIFUDA'S SON IS.
I DON'T THINK HE'S READY.
THAT IS FOR ME TO DECIDE.

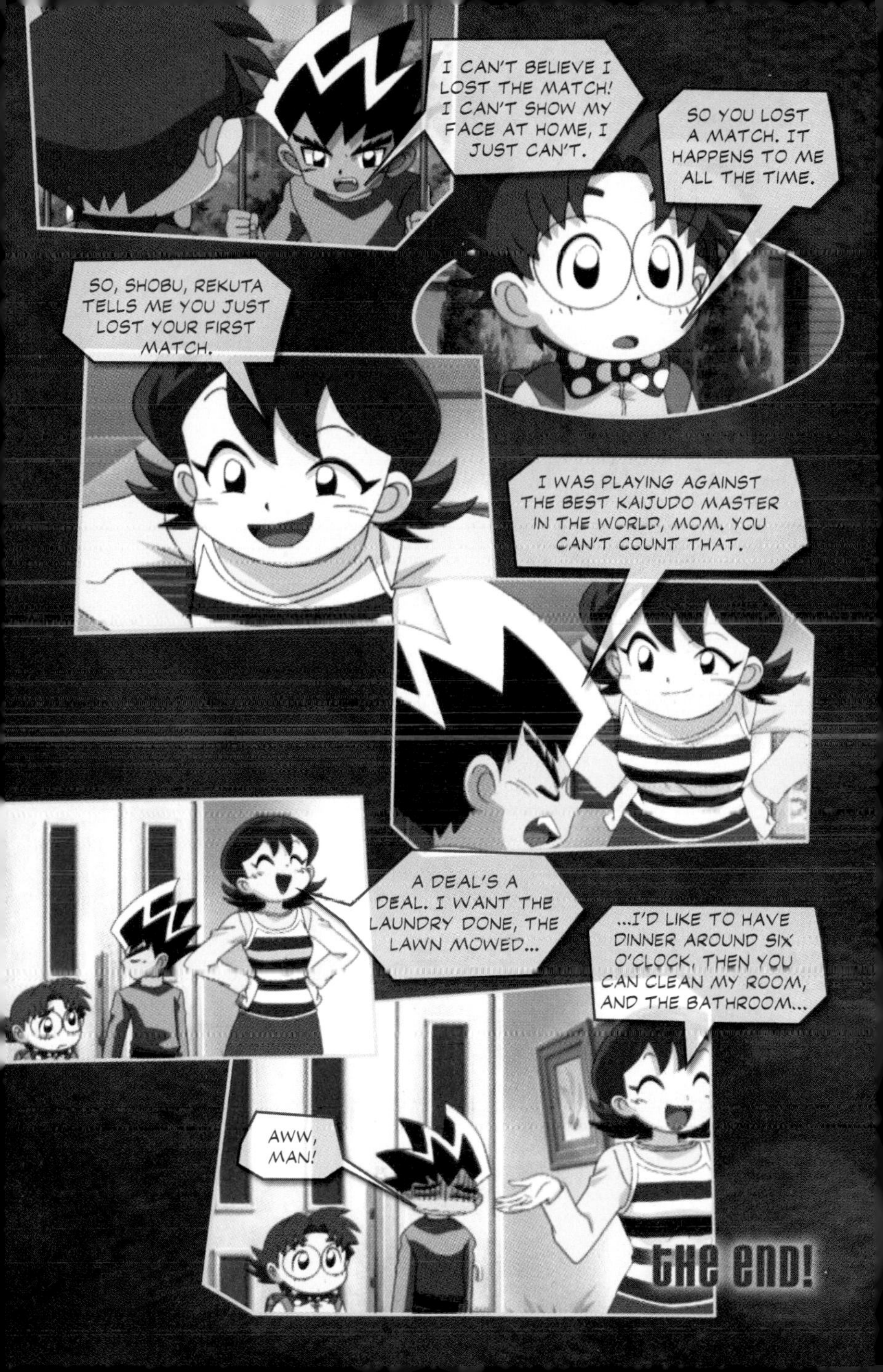

I CAN'T BELIEVE I LOST THE MATCH! I CAN'T SHOW MY FACE AT HOME, I JUST CAN'T.
SO YOU LOST A MATCH. IT HAPPENS TO ME ALL THE TIME.
SO, SHOBU, REKUTA TELLS ME YOU JUST LOST YOUR FIRST MATCH.
I WAS PLAYING AGAINST THE BEST KAIJUDO MASTER IN THE WORLD, MOM. YOU CAN'T COUNT THAT.
A DEAL'S A DEAL. I WANT THE LAUNDRY DONE, THE LAWN MOWED...
...I'D LIKE TO HAVE DINNER AROUND SIX O'CLOCK, THEN YOU CAN CLEAN MY ROOM, AND THE BATHROOM...
AWW, MAN!
THE END!

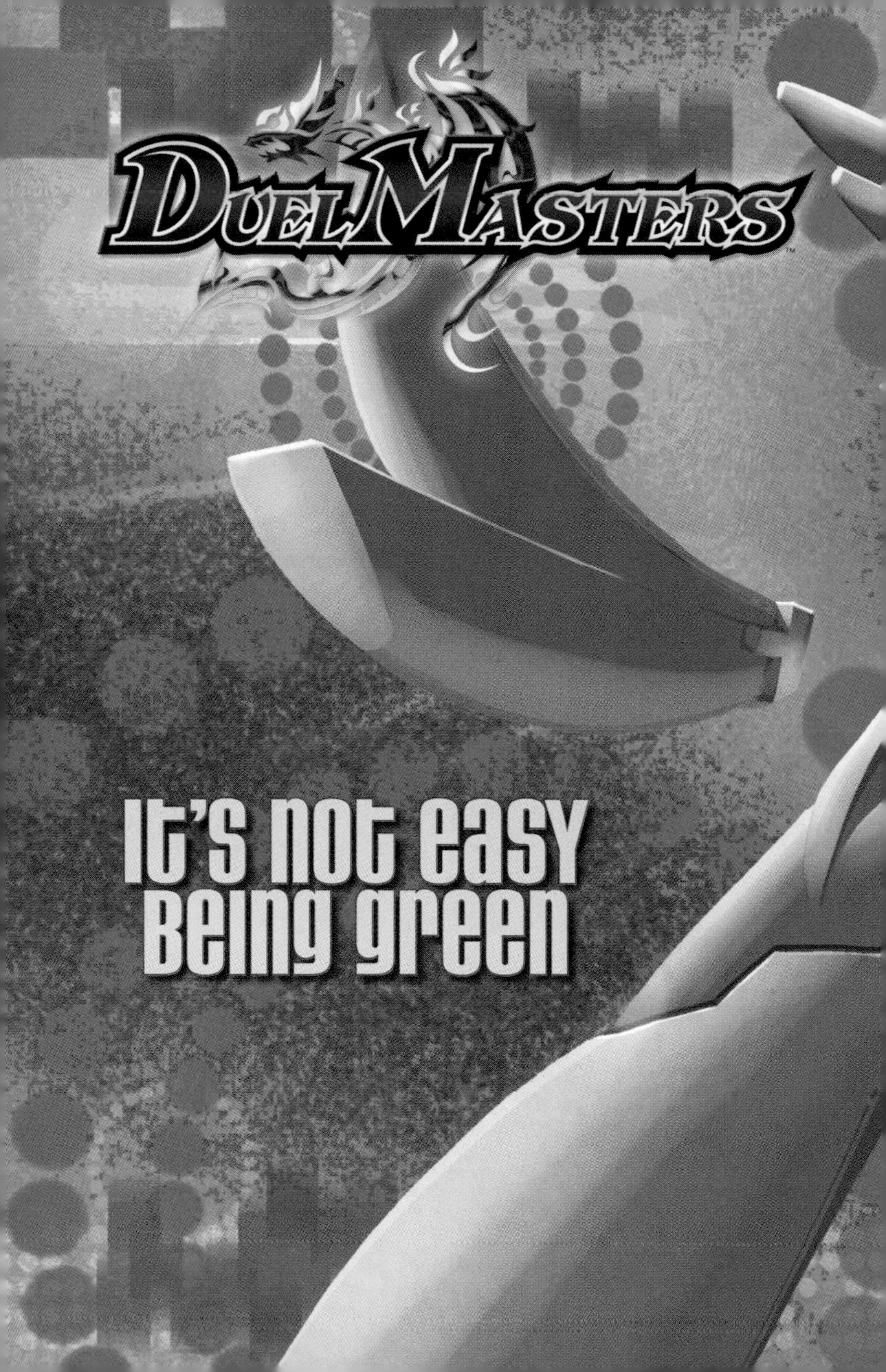
Duel Masters™
It's not easy
Being green

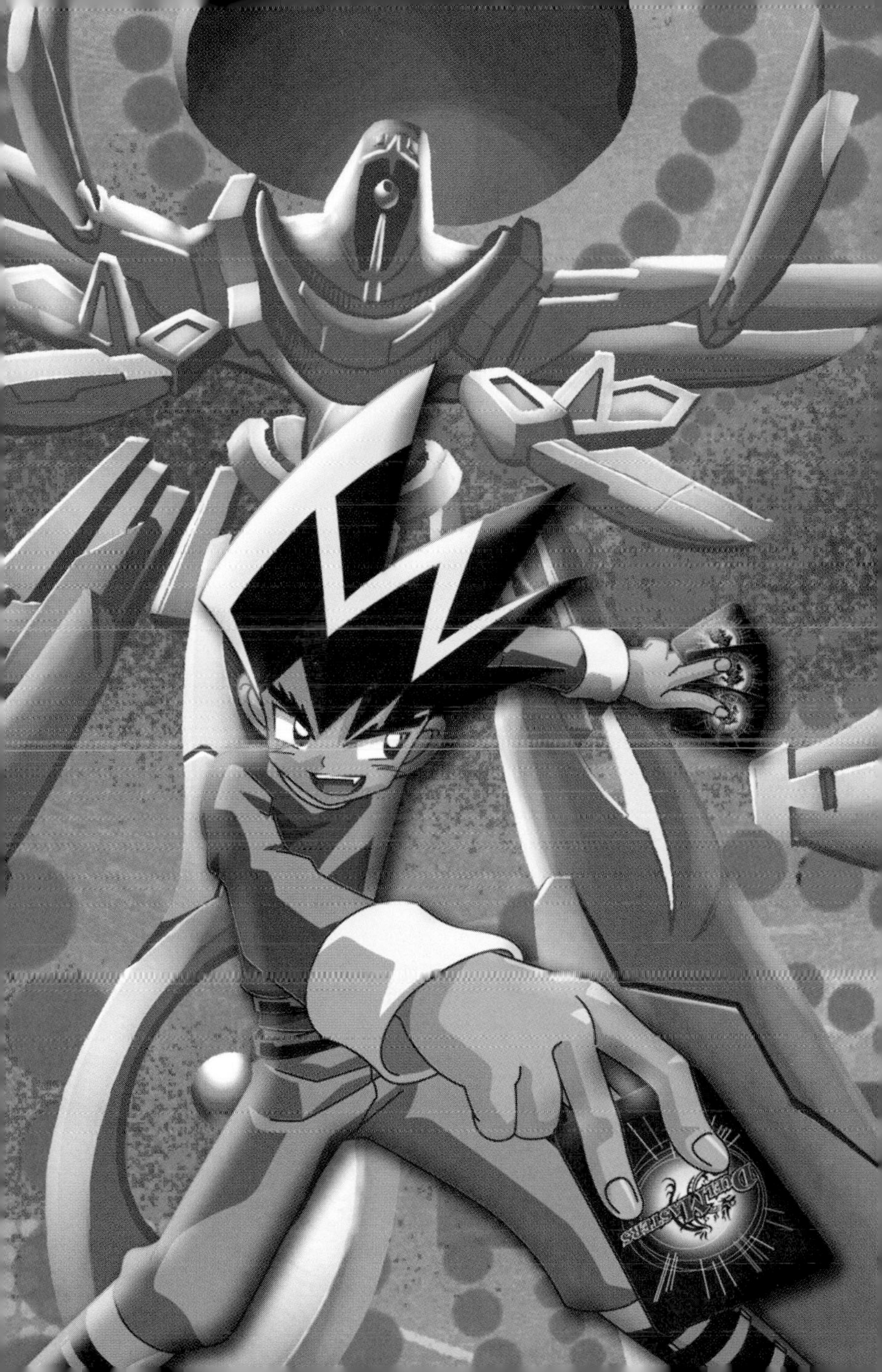

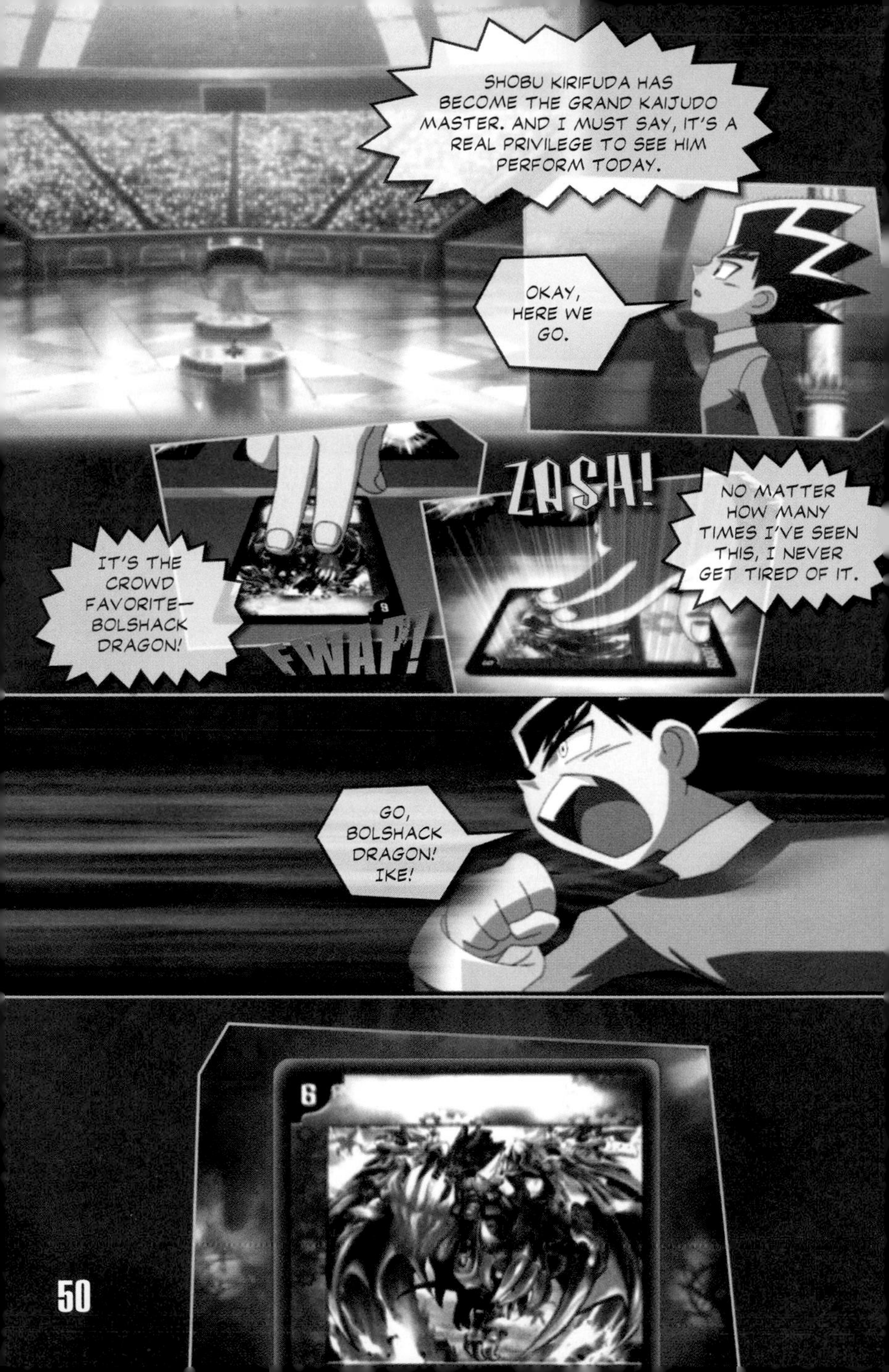
SHOBU KIRIFUDA HAS BECOME THE GRAND KAIJUDO MASTER. AND I MUST SAY, IT'S A REAL PRIVILEGE TO SEE HIM PERFORM TODAY.
OKAY, HERE WE GO.
IT'S THE CROWD FAVORITE—BOLSHACK DRAGON!
FWAP!
ZASH!
NO MATTER HOW MANY TIMES I'VE SEEN THIS, I NEVER GET TIRED OF IT.
GO, BOLSHACK DRAGON! IKE!

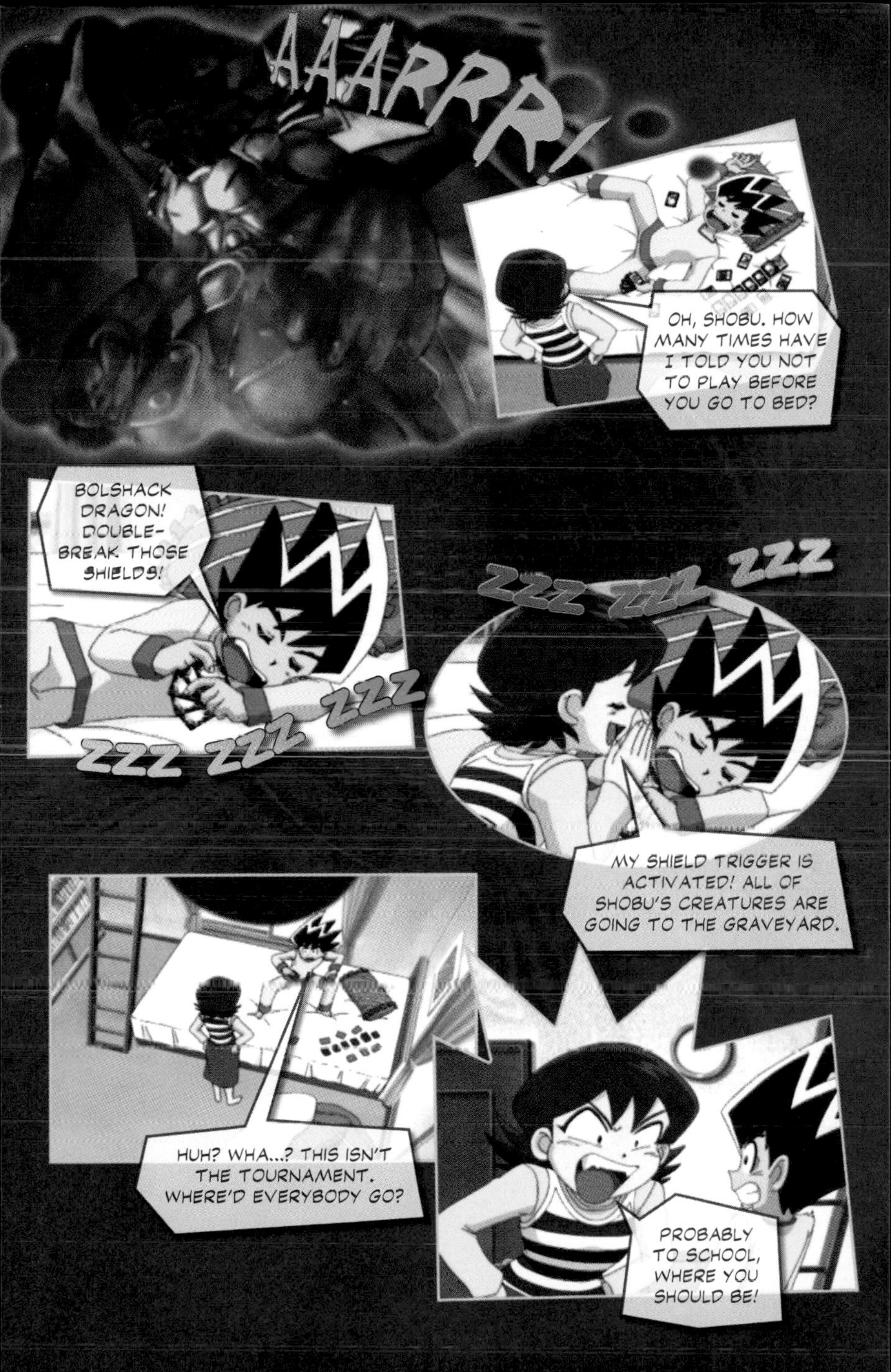
AAARRR!
OH, SHOBU. HOW MANY TIMES HAVE I TOLD YOU NOT TO PLAY BEFORE YOU GO TO BED?
BOLSHACK DRAGON! DOUBLE-BREAK THOSE SHIELDS!
ZZZ ZZZ ZZZ
ZZZ ZZZ ZZZ
MY SHIELD TRIGGER IS ACTIVATED! ALL OF SHOBU'S CREATURES ARE GOING TO THE GRAVEYARD.
HUH? WHA...? THIS ISN'T THE TOURNAMENT. WHERE'D EVERYBODY GO?
PROBABLY TO SCHOOL, WHERE YOU SHOULD BE!

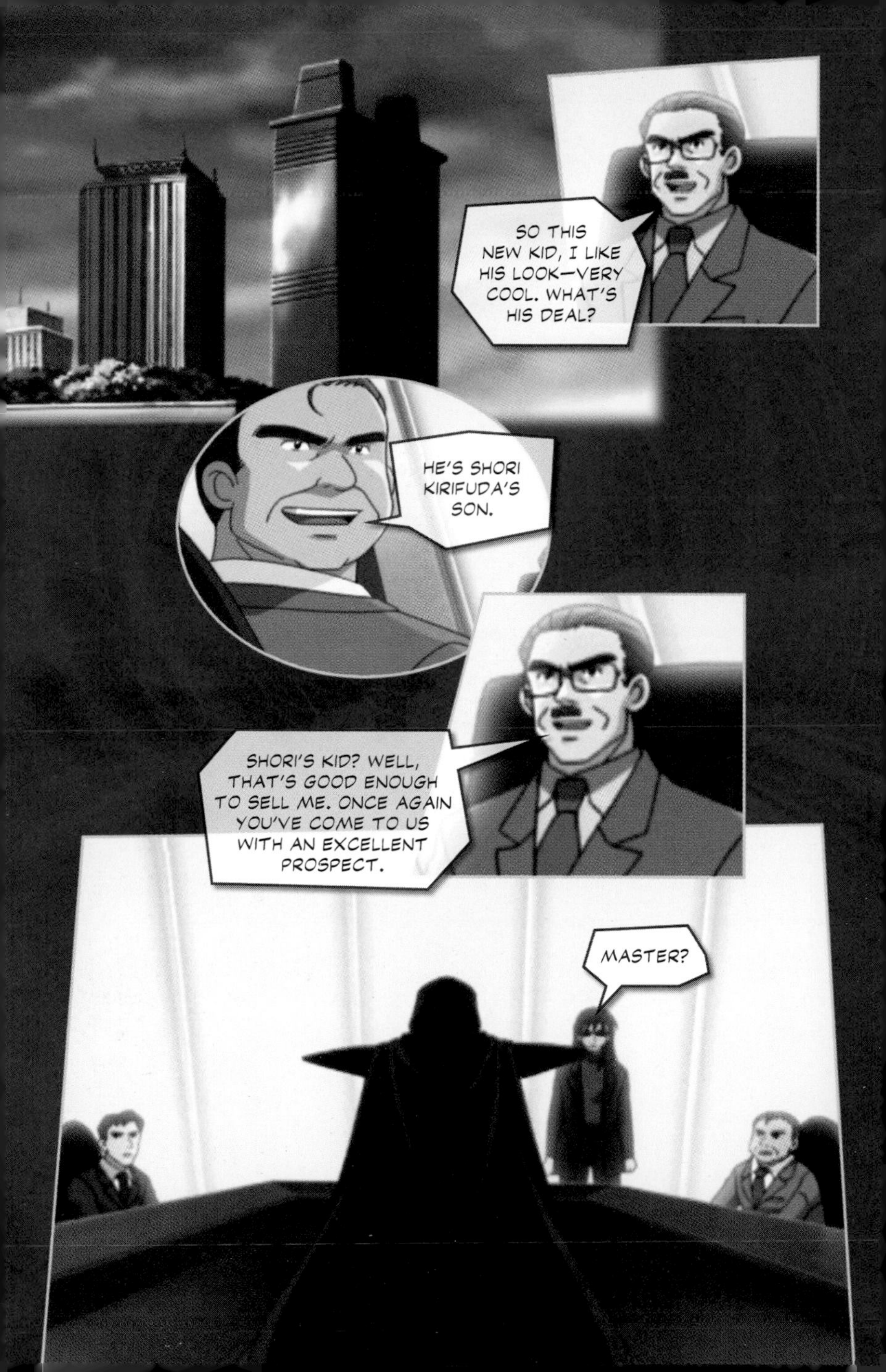
SO THIS NEW KID, I LIKE HIS LOOK—VERY COOL. WHAT'S HIS DEAL?
HE'S SHORI KIRIFUDA'S SON.
SHORI'S KID? WELL, THAT'S GOOD ENOUGH TO SELL ME. ONCE AGAIN YOU'VE COME TO US WITH AN EXCELLENT PROSPECT.
MASTER?

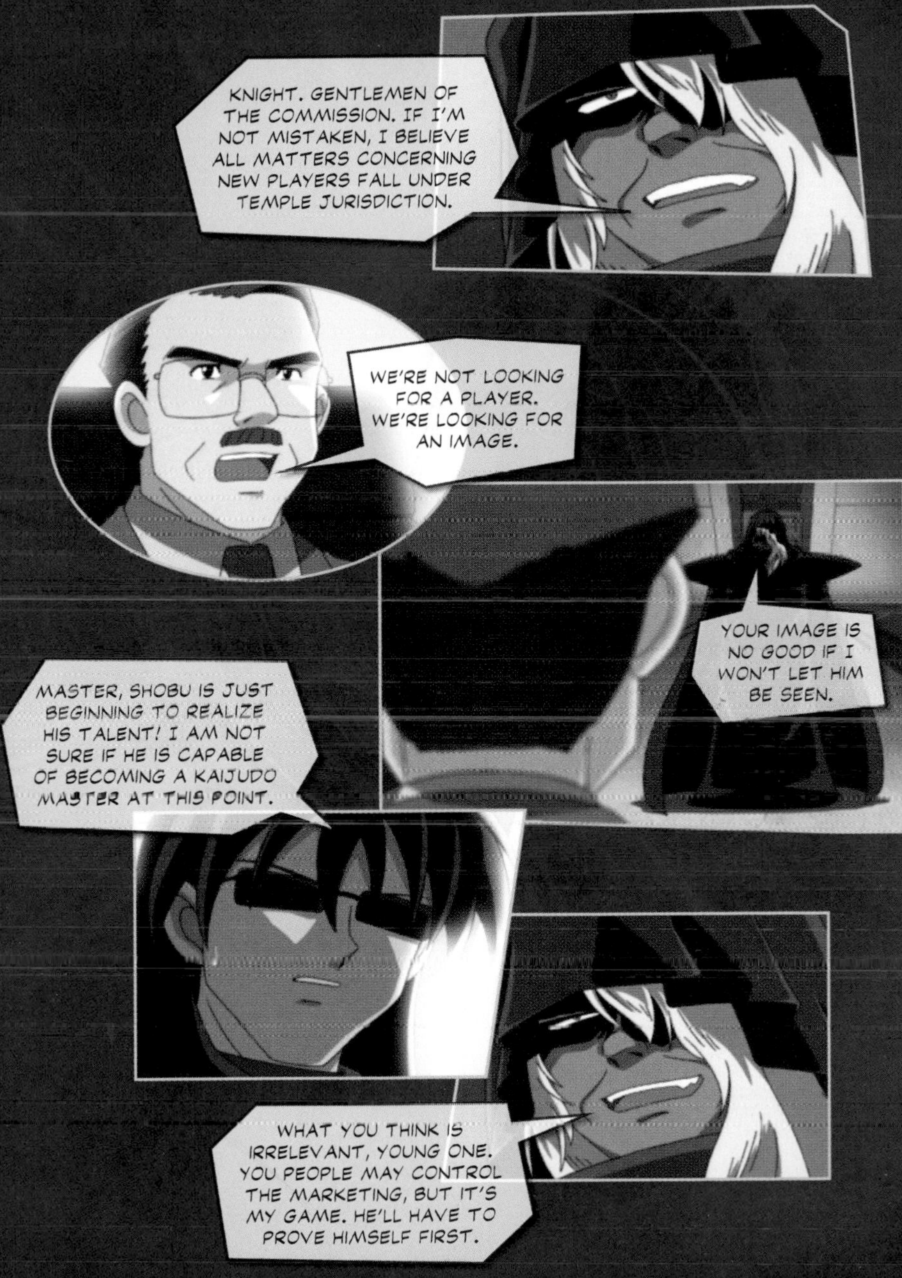
KNIGHT. GENTLEMEN OF THE COMMISSION. IF I'M NOT MISTAKEN, I BELIEVE ALL MATTERS CONCERNING NEW PLAYERS FALL UNDER TEMPLE JURISDICTION.
WE'RE NOT LOOKING FOR A PLAYER. WE'RE LOOKING FOR AN IMAGE.
YOUR IMAGE IS NO GOOD IF I WON'T LET HIM BE SEEN.
MASTER, SHOBU IS JUST BEGINNING TO REALIZE HIS TALENT! I AM NOT SURE IF HE IS CAPABLE OF BECOMING A KAIJUDO MASTER AT THIS POINT.
WHAT YOU THINK IS IRRELEVANT, YOUNG ONE. YOU PEOPLE MAY CONTROL THE MARKETING, BUT IT'S MY GAME. HE'LL HAVE TO PROVE HIMSELF FIRST.

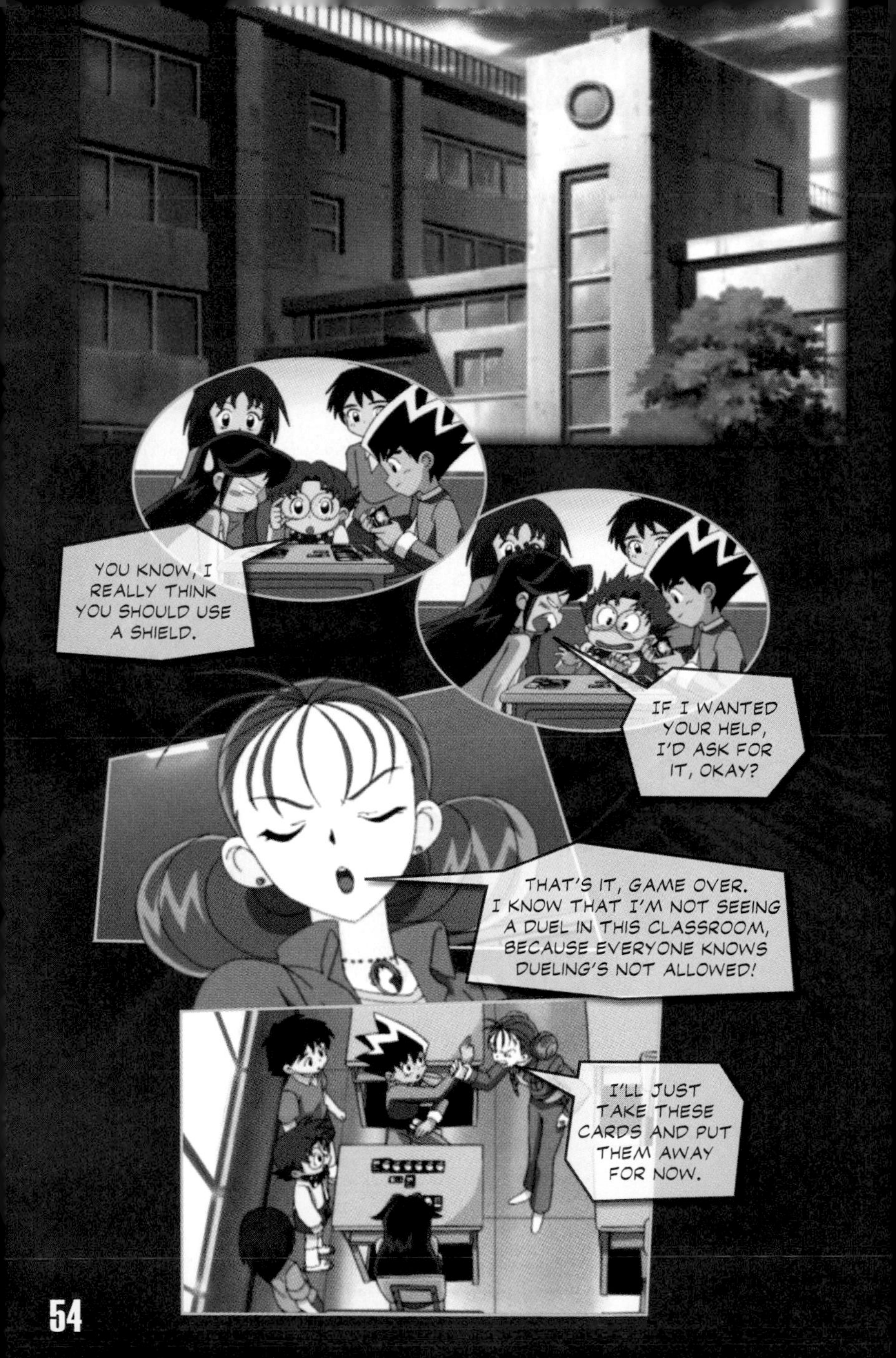
YOU KNOW, I REALLY THINK YOU SHOULD USE A SHIELD.
IF I WANTED YOUR HELP, I'D ASK FOR IT, OKAY?
THAT'S IT, GAME OVER. I KNOW THAT I'M NOT SEEING A DUEL IN THIS CLASSROOM, BECAUSE EVERYONE KNOWS DUELING'S NOT ALLOWED!
I'LL JUST TAKE THESE CARDS AND PUT THEM AWAY FOR NOW.

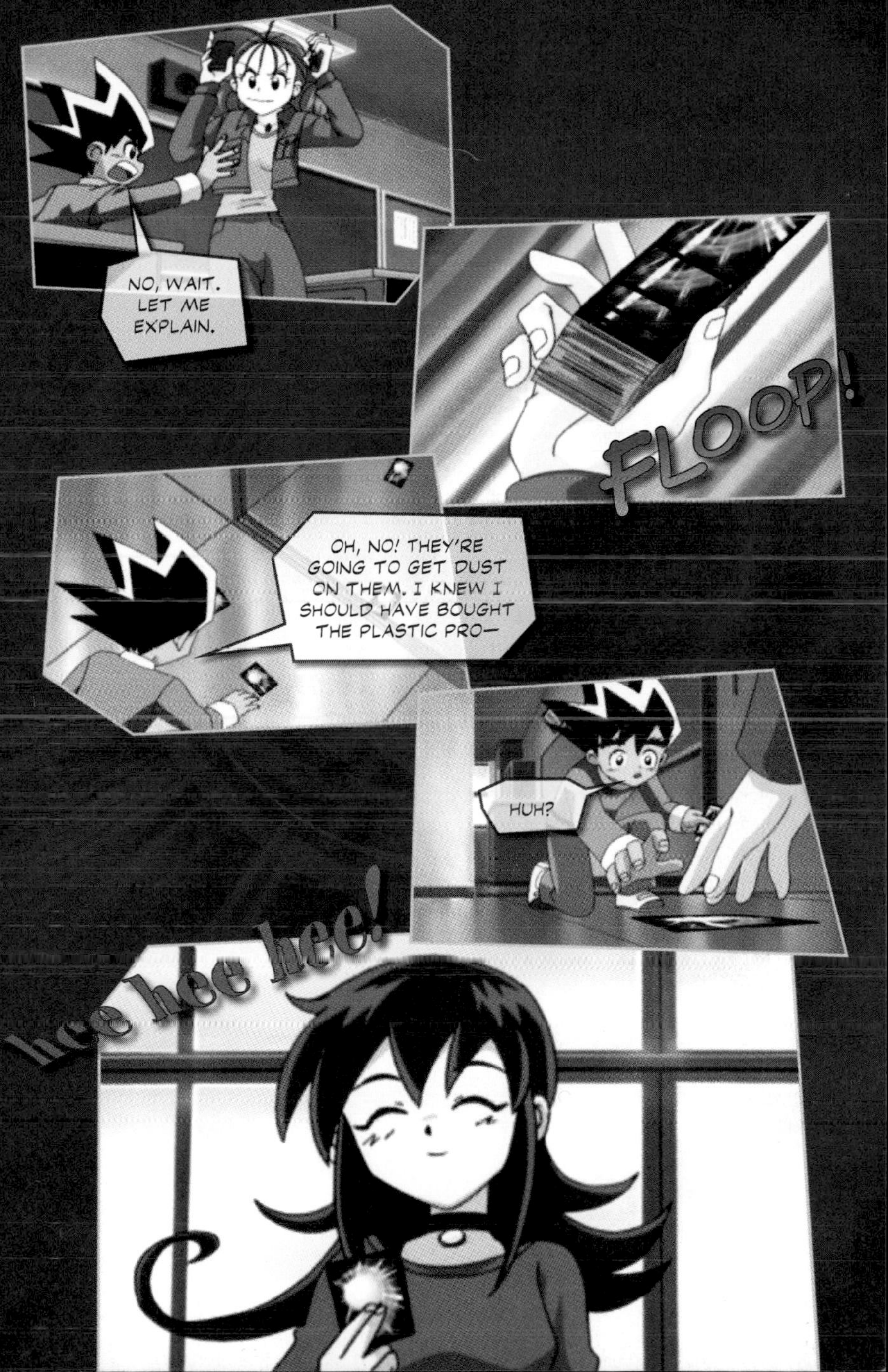
NO, WAIT. LET ME EXPLAIN.
FLOOP!
OH, NO! THEY'RE GOING TO GET DUST ON THEM. I KNEW I SHOULD HAVE BOUGHT THE PLASTIC PRO—
HUH?
hee hee hee!

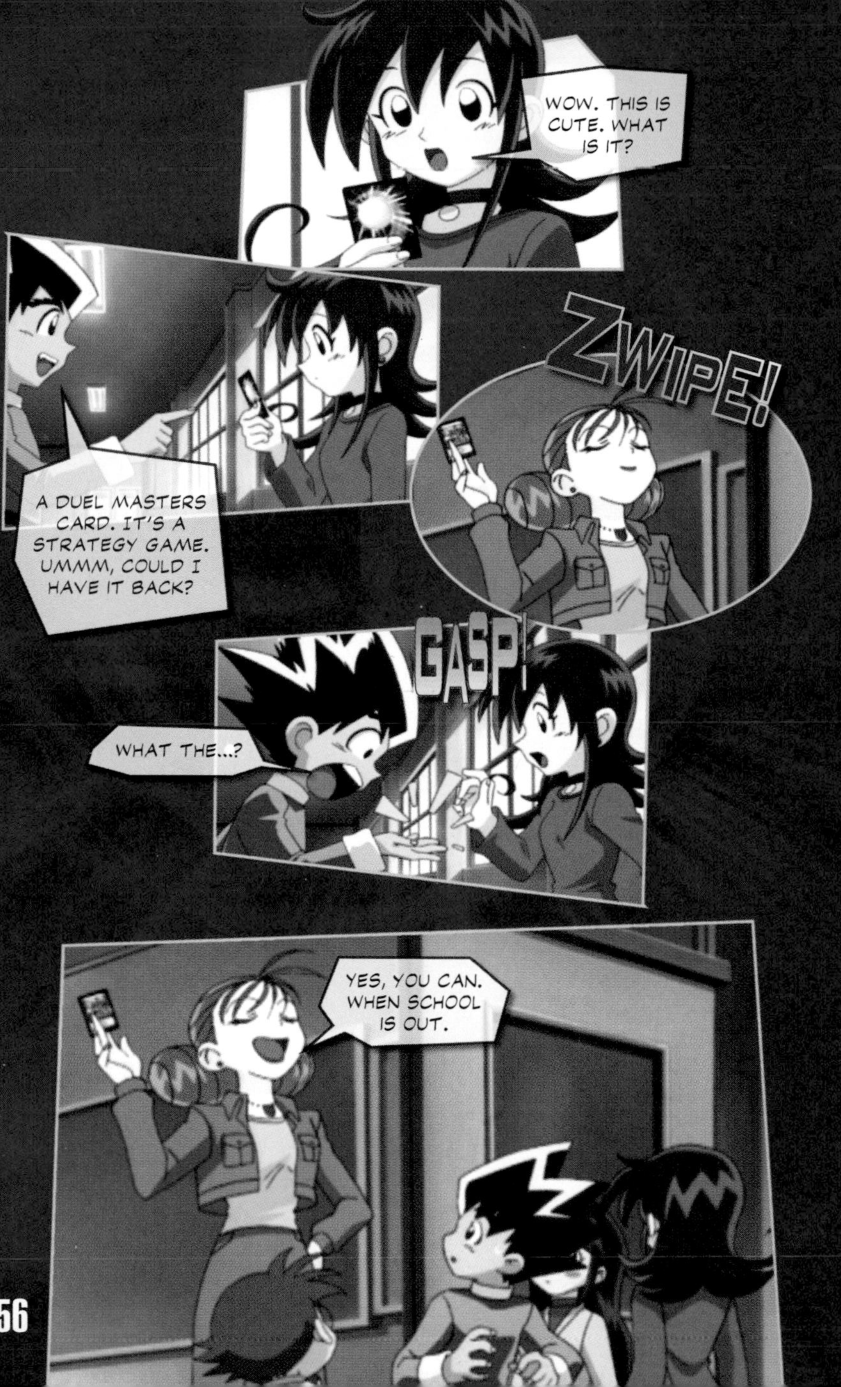
WOW. THIS IS CUTE. WHAT IS IT?
A DUEL MASTERS CARD. IT'S A STRATEGY GAME. UMMM, COULD I HAVE IT BACK?
ZWIPE!
GASP!
WHAT THE...?
YES, YOU CAN. WHEN SCHOOL IS OUT.

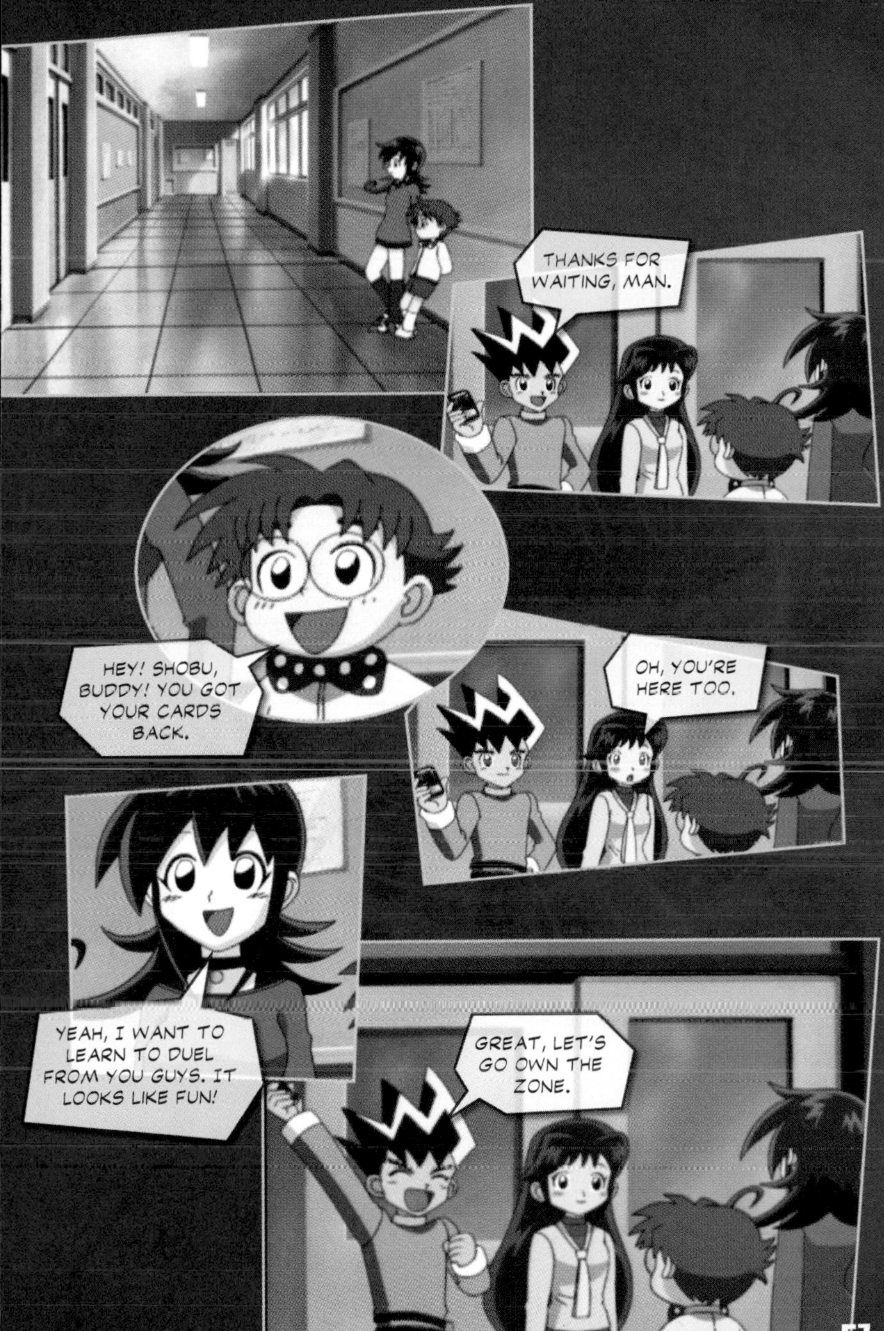
THANKS FOR WAITING, MAN.
HEY! SHOBU, BUDDY! YOU GOT YOUR CARDS BACK.
OH, YOU'RE HERE TOO.
YEAH, I WANT TO LEARN TO DUEL FROM YOU GUYS. IT LOOKS LIKE FUN!
GREAT, LET'S GO OWN THE ZONE.

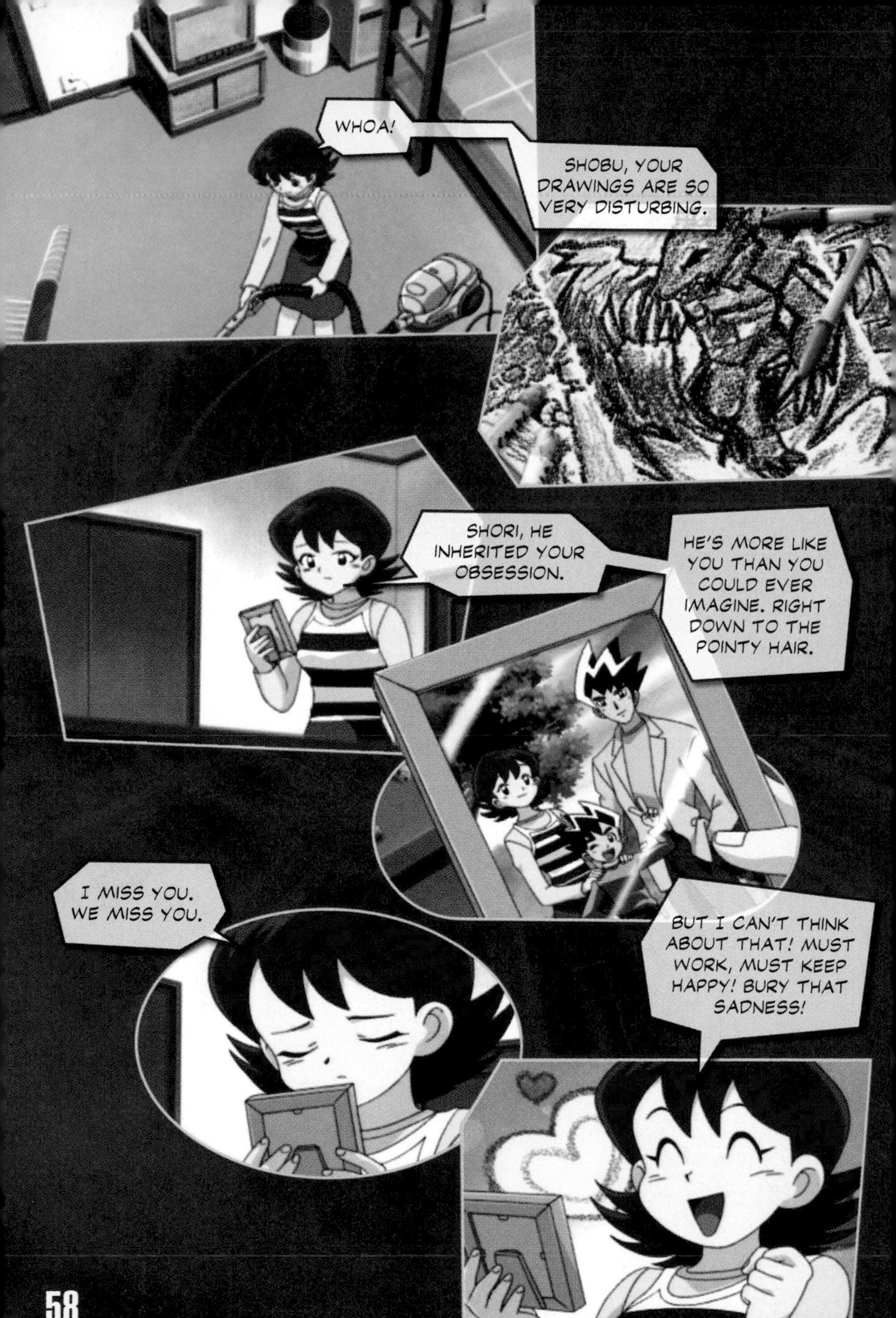
WHOA!
SHOBU, YOUR DRAWINGS ARE SO VERY DISTURBING.
SHORI, HE INHERITED YOUR OBSESSION.
HE'S MORE LIKE YOU THAN YOU COULD EVER IMAGINE. RIGHT DOWN TO THE POINTY HAIR.
I MISS YOU. WE MISS YOU.
BUT I CAN'T THINK ABOUT THAT! MUST WORK, MUST KEEP HAPPY! BURY THAT SADNESS!

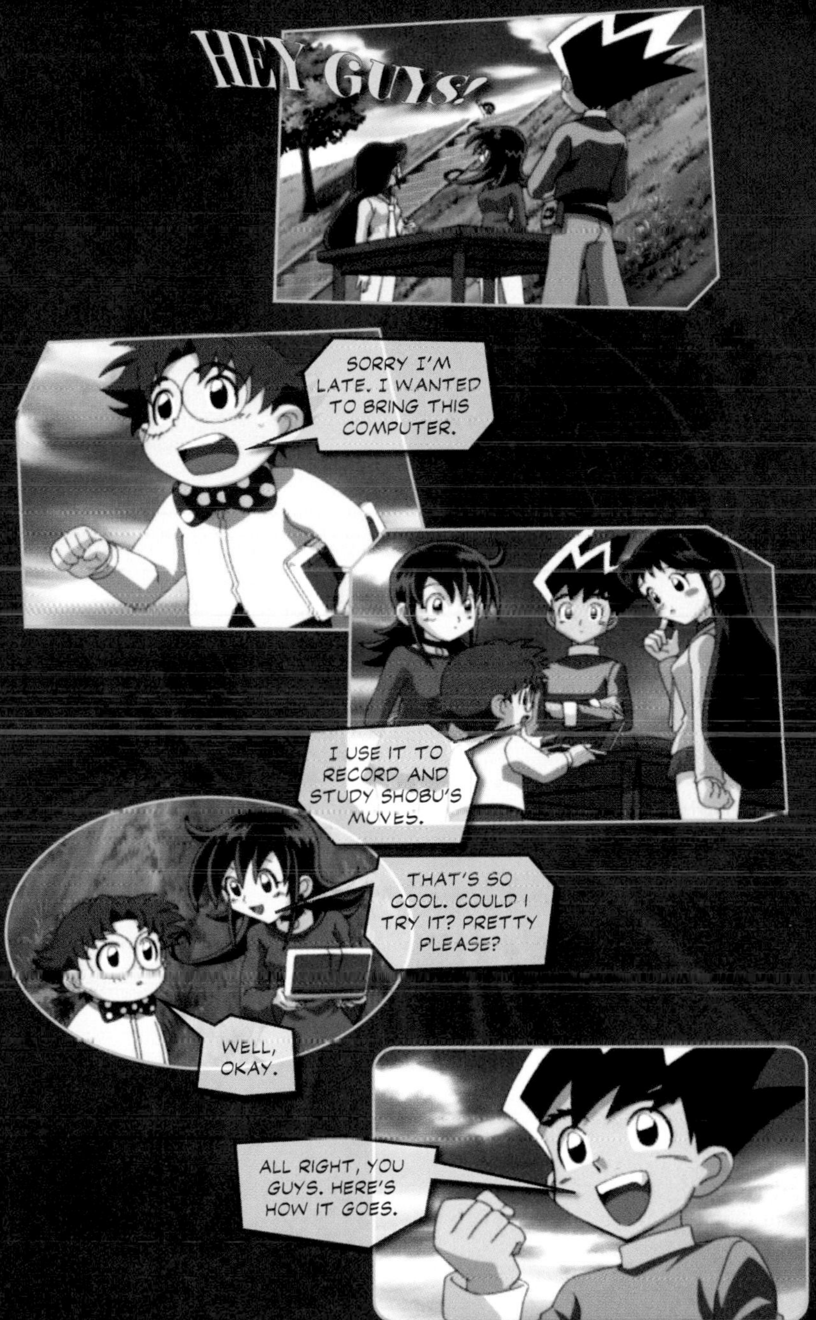
HEY GUYS!
SORRY I'M LATE. I WANTED TO BRING THIS COMPUTER.
I USE IT TO RECORD AND STUDY SHOBU'S MOVES.
THAT'S SO COOL. COULD I TRY IT? PRETTY PLEASE?
WELL, OKAY.
ALL RIGHT, YOU GUYS. HERE'S HOW IT GOES.

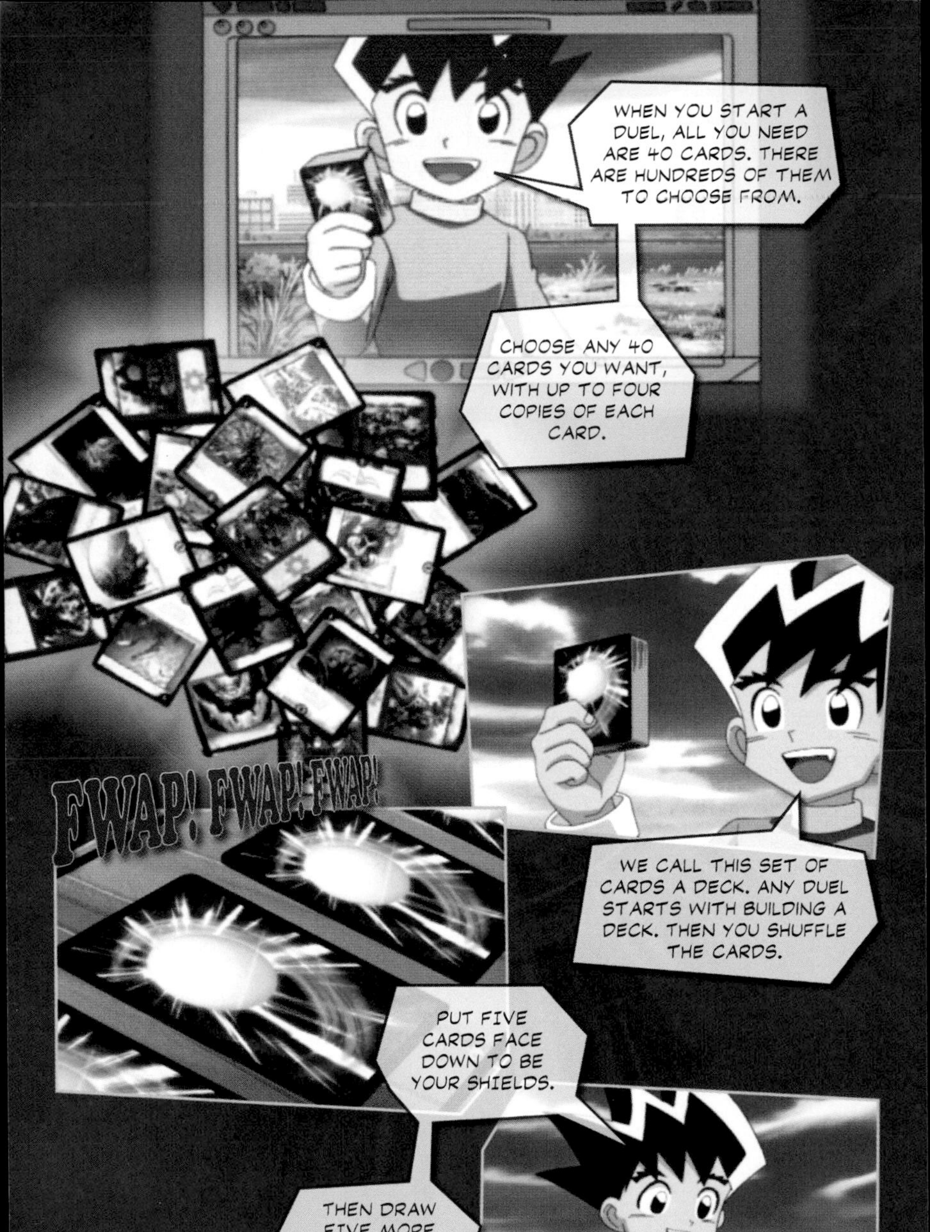
WHEN YOU START A DUEL, ALL YOU NEED ARE 40 CARDS. THERE ARE HUNDREDS OF THEM TO CHOOSE FROM.
CHOOSE ANY 40 CARDS YOU WANT, WITH UP TO FOUR COPIES OF EACH CARD.
WE CALL THIS SET OF CARDS A DECK. ANY DUEL STARTS WITH BUILDING A DECK. THEN YOU SHUFFLE THE CARDS.
FWAP! FWAP! FWAP!
PUT FIVE CARDS FACE DOWN TO BE YOUR SHIELDS.
THEN DRAW FIVE MORE CARDS. THIS IS YOUR HAND.

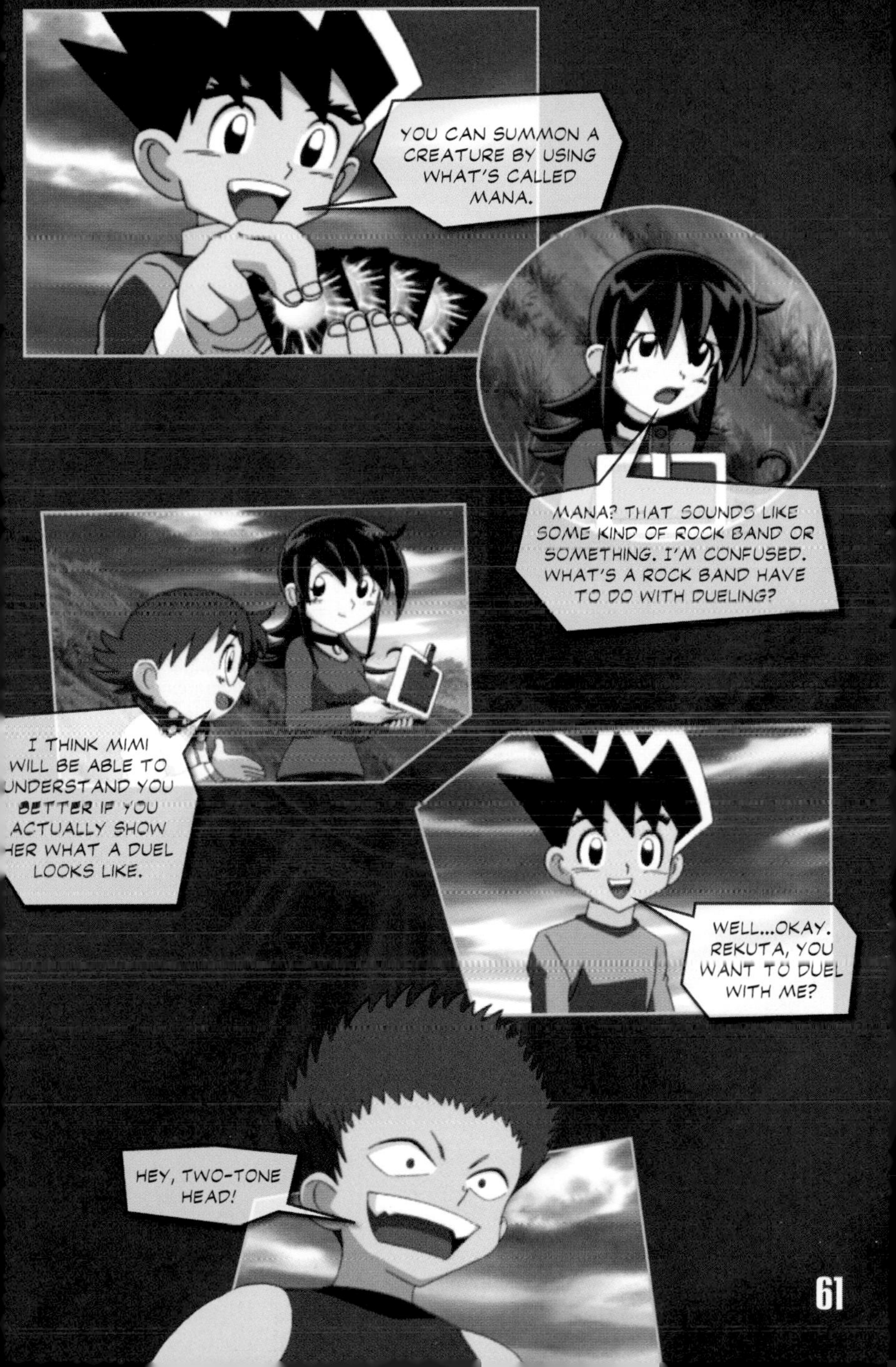
YOU CAN SUMMON A CREATURE BY USING WHAT'S CALLED MANA.
MANA? THAT SOUNDS LIKE SOME KIND OF ROCK BAND OR SOMETHING. I'M CONFUSED. WHAT'S A ROCK BAND HAVE TO DO WITH DUELING?
I THINK MIMI WILL BE ABLE TO UNDERSTAND YOU BETTER IF YOU ACTUALLY SHOW HER WHAT A DUEL LOOKS LIKE.
WELL...OKAY. REKUTA, YOU WANT TO DUEL WITH ME?
HEY, TWO-TONE HEAD!

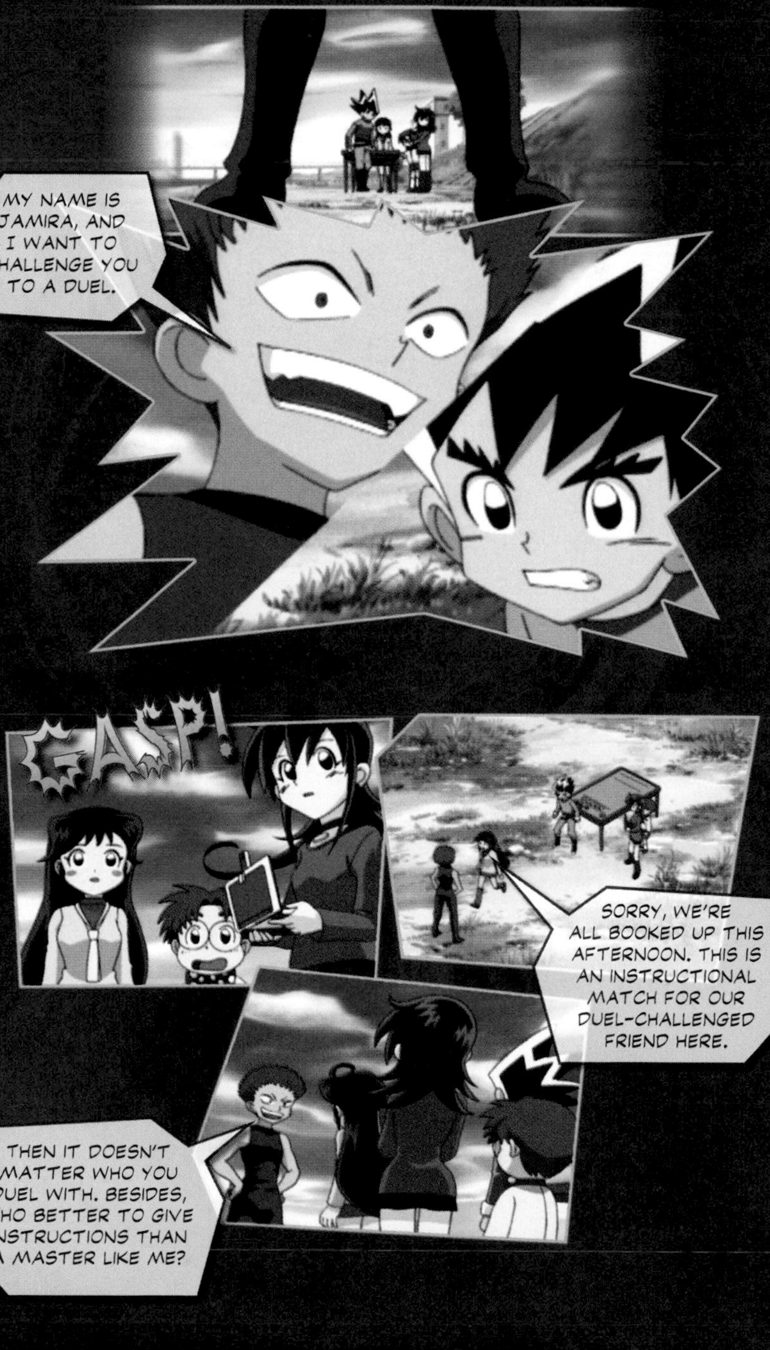
MY NAME IS JAMIRA, AND I WANT TO CHALLENGE YOU TO A DUEL.
GASP!
SORRY, WE'RE ALL BOOKED UP THIS AFTERNOON. THIS IS AN INSTRUCTIONAL MATCH FOR OUR DUEL-CHALLENGED FRIEND HERE.
THEN IT DOESN'T MATTER WHO YOU DUEL WITH. BESIDES, WHO BETTER TO GIVE INSTRUCTIONS THAN A MASTER LIKE ME?

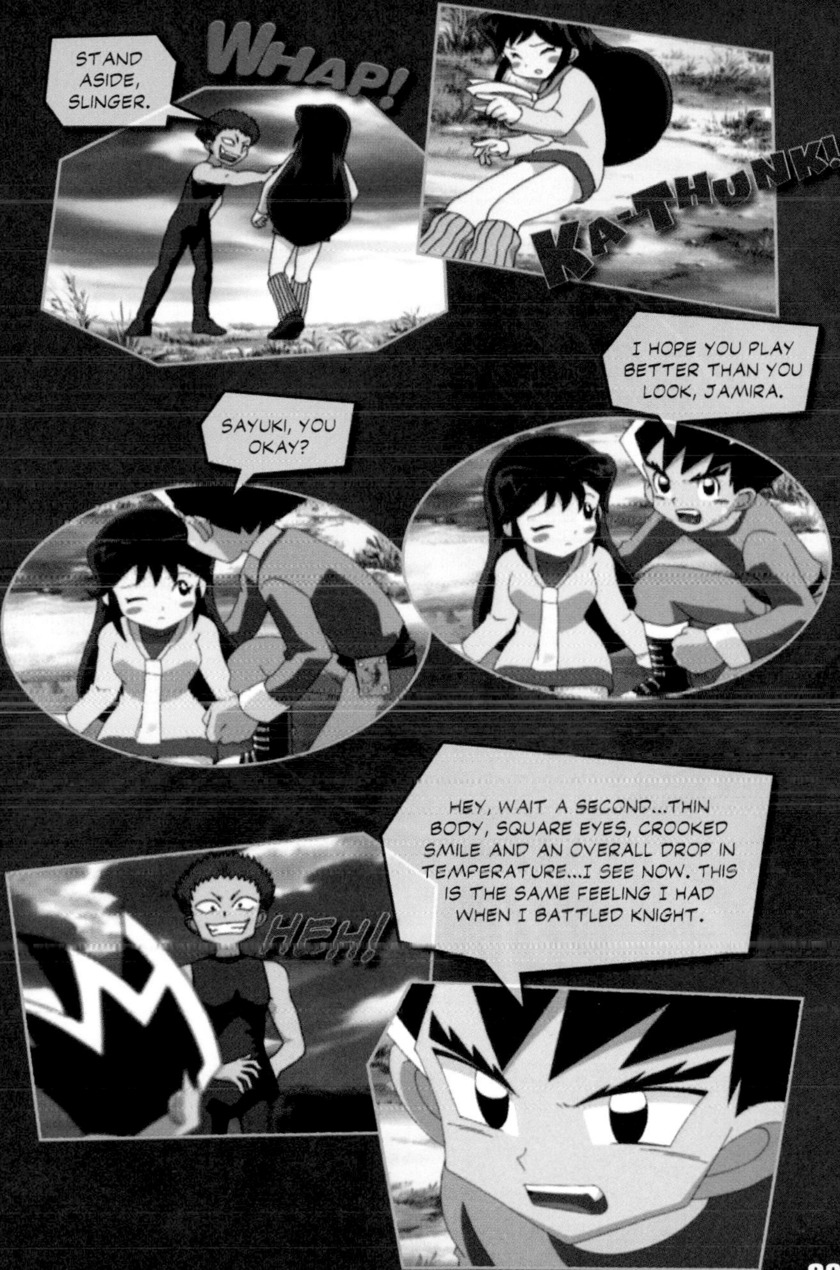
STAND ASIDE, SLINGER.
WHAP!
KA-THUNK!
I HOPE YOU PLAY BETTER THAN YOU LOOK, JAMIRA.
SAYUKI, YOU OKAY?
HEY, WAIT A SECOND...THIN BODY, SQUARE EYES, CROOKED SMILE AND AN OVERALL DROP IN TEMPERATURE...I SEE NOW. THIS IS THE SAME FEELING I HAD WHEN I BATTLED KNIGHT.
HEH!

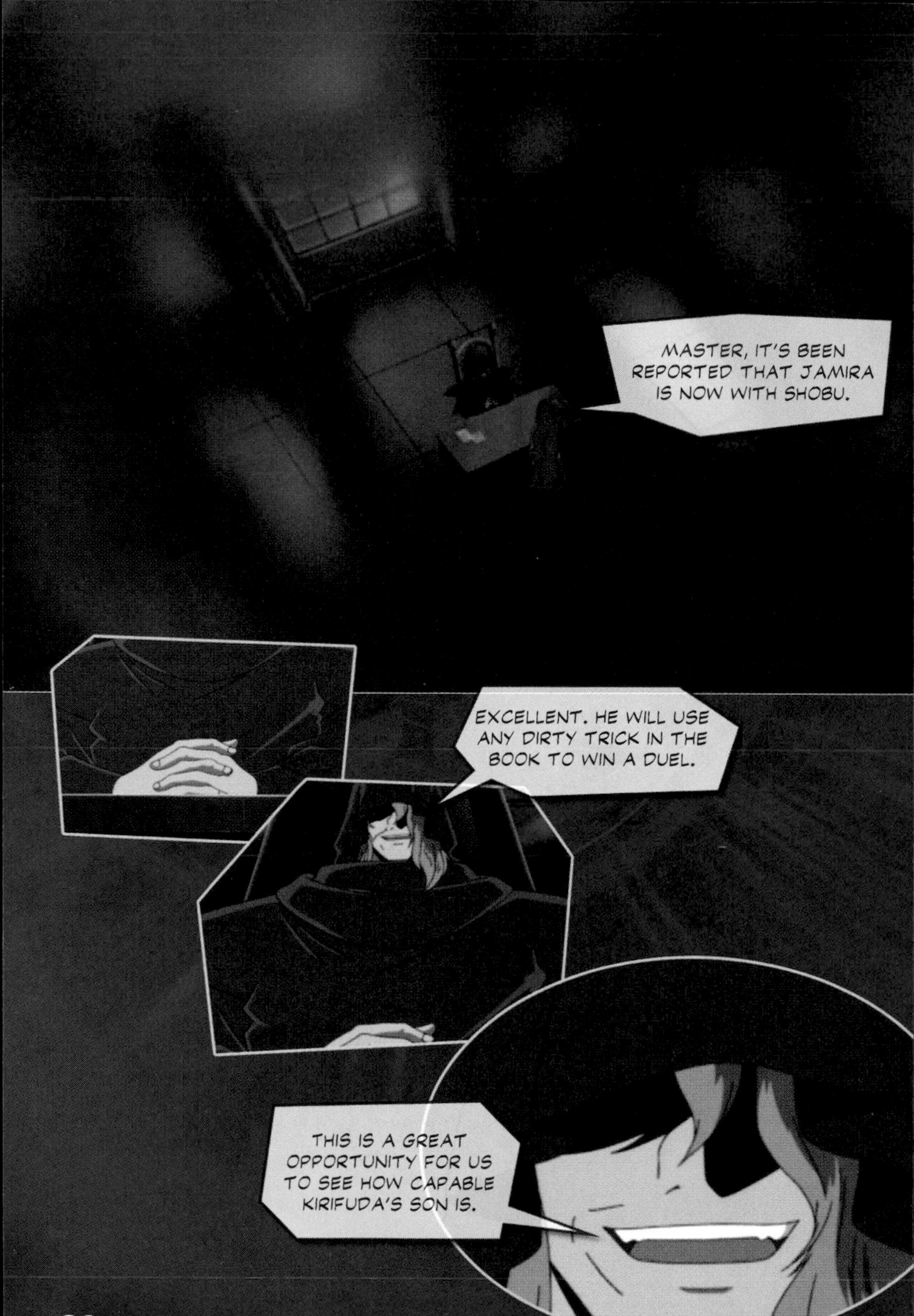
MASTER, IT'S BEEN REPORTED THAT JAMIRA IS NOW WITH SHOBU.
EXCELLENT. HE WILL USE ANY DIRTY TRICK IN THE BOOK TO WIN A DUEL.
THIS IS A GREAT OPPORTUNITY FOR US TO SEE HOW CAPABLE KIRIFUDA'S SON IS.

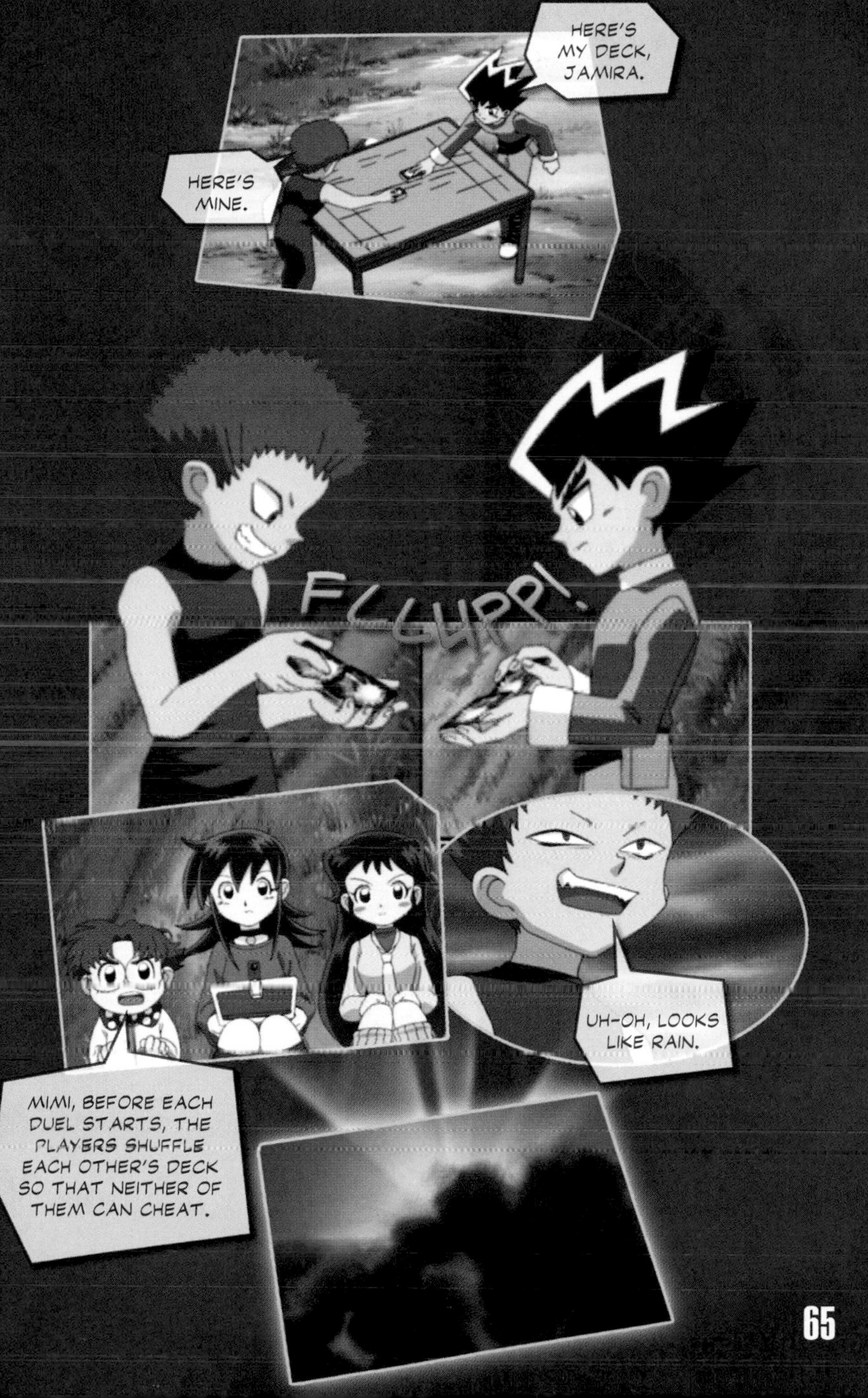

HERE'S MY DECK, JAMIRA.
HERE'S MINE.
FLLUPP!
UH-OH, LOOKS LIKE RAIN.
MIMI, BEFORE EACH DUEL STARTS, THE PLAYERS SHUFFLE EACH OTHER'S DECK SO THAT NEITHER OF THEM CAN CHEAT.

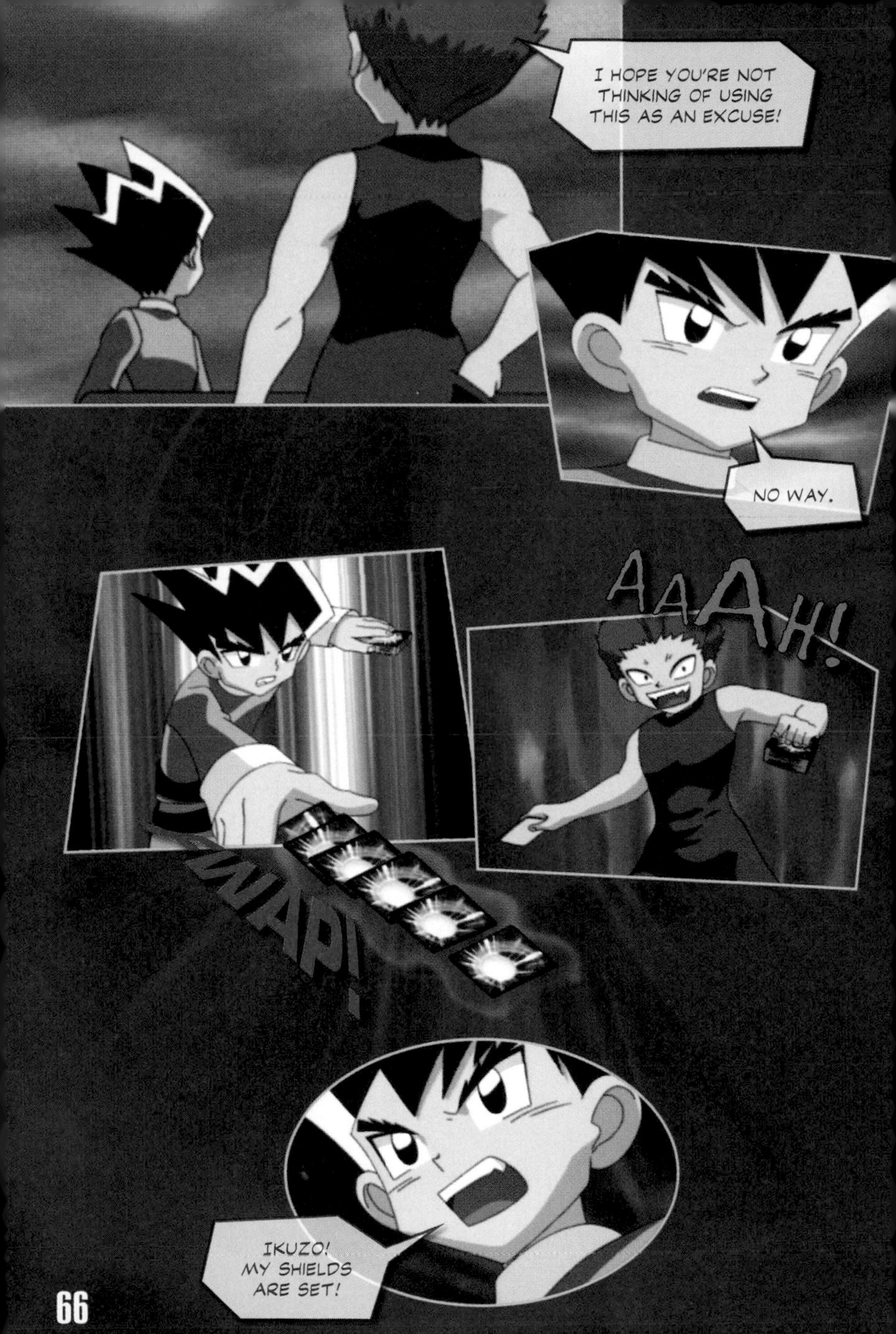
I HOPE YOU'RE NOT THINKING OF USING THIS AS AN EXCUSE!
NO WAY.
AAAH!
SWAP!
IKUZO! MY SHIELDS ARE SET!

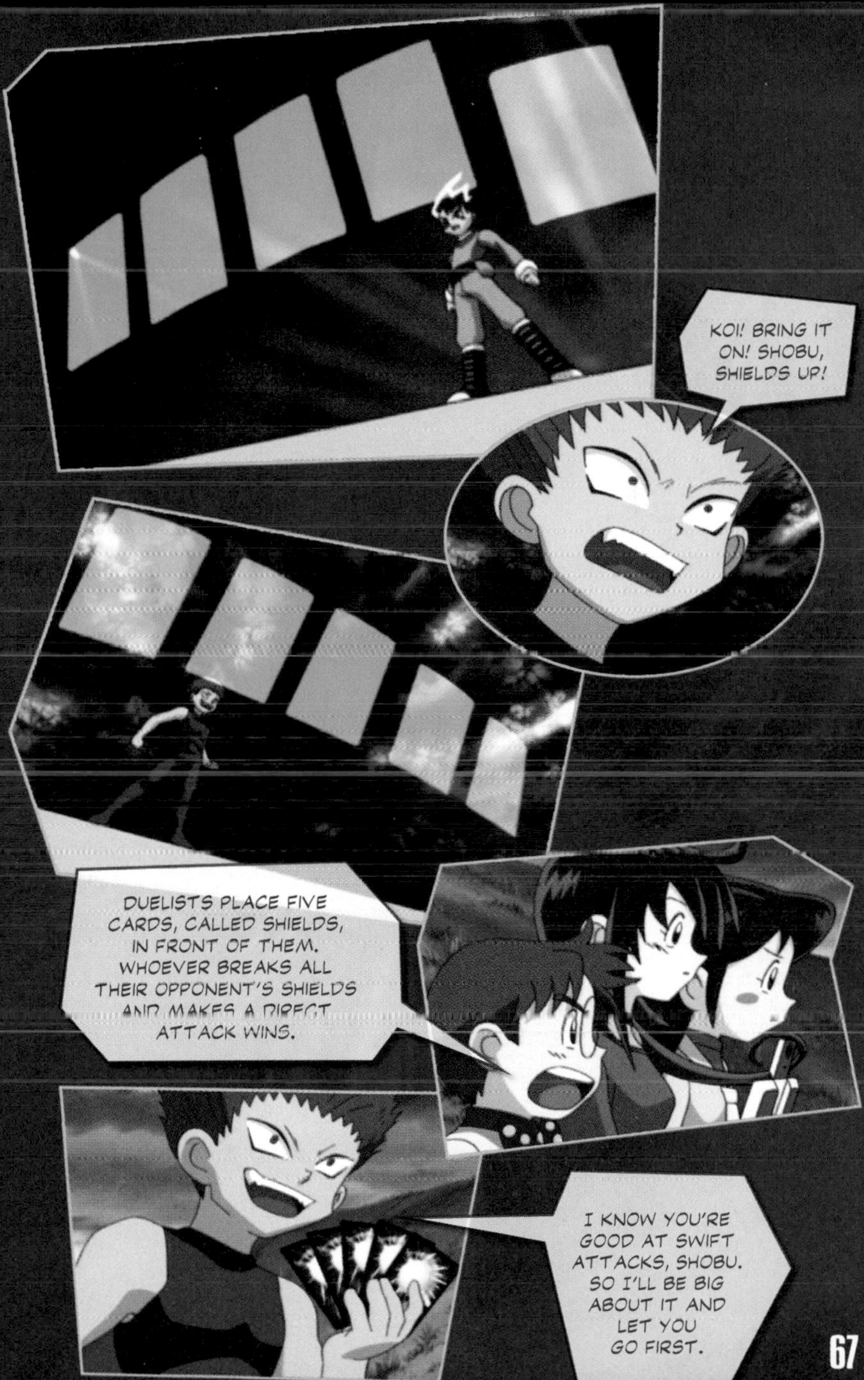
KOI! BRING IT ON! SHOBU, SHIELDS UP!
DUELISTS PLACE FIVE CARDS, CALLED SHIELDS, IN FRONT OF THEM. WHOEVER BREAKS ALL THEIR OPPONENT'S SHIELDS AND MAKES A DIRECT ATTACK WINS.
I KNOW YOU'RE GOOD AT SWIFT ATTACKS, SHOBU. SO I'LL BE BIG ABOUT IT AND LET YOU GO FIRST.

YOU'RE GOING TO REGRET THAT LATER, JAMIRA.

ONLY CREATURES ARE CAPABLE OF ATTACKING YOUR OPPONENT. AND YOU HAVE TO HAVE ENOUGH MANA TO SUMMON A CREATURE.

KOI!

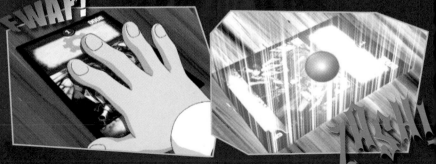

FWAP!

TASH!

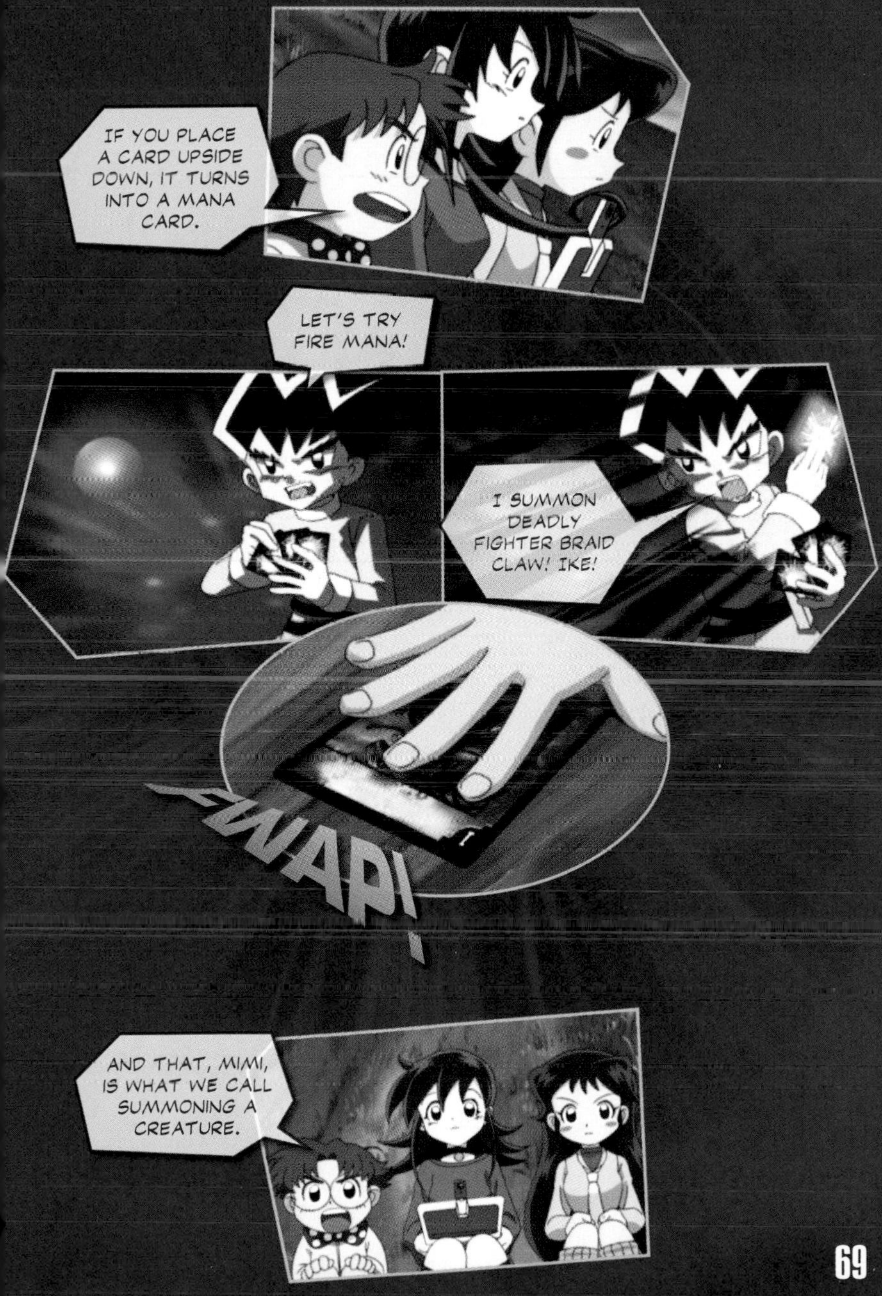
IF YOU PLACE A CARD UPSIDE DOWN, IT TURNS INTO A MANA CARD.
LET'S TRY FIRE MANA!
I SUMMON DEADLY FIGHTER BRAID CLAW! IKE!
FWAP!
AND THAT, MIMI, IS WHAT WE CALL SUMMONING A CREATURE.

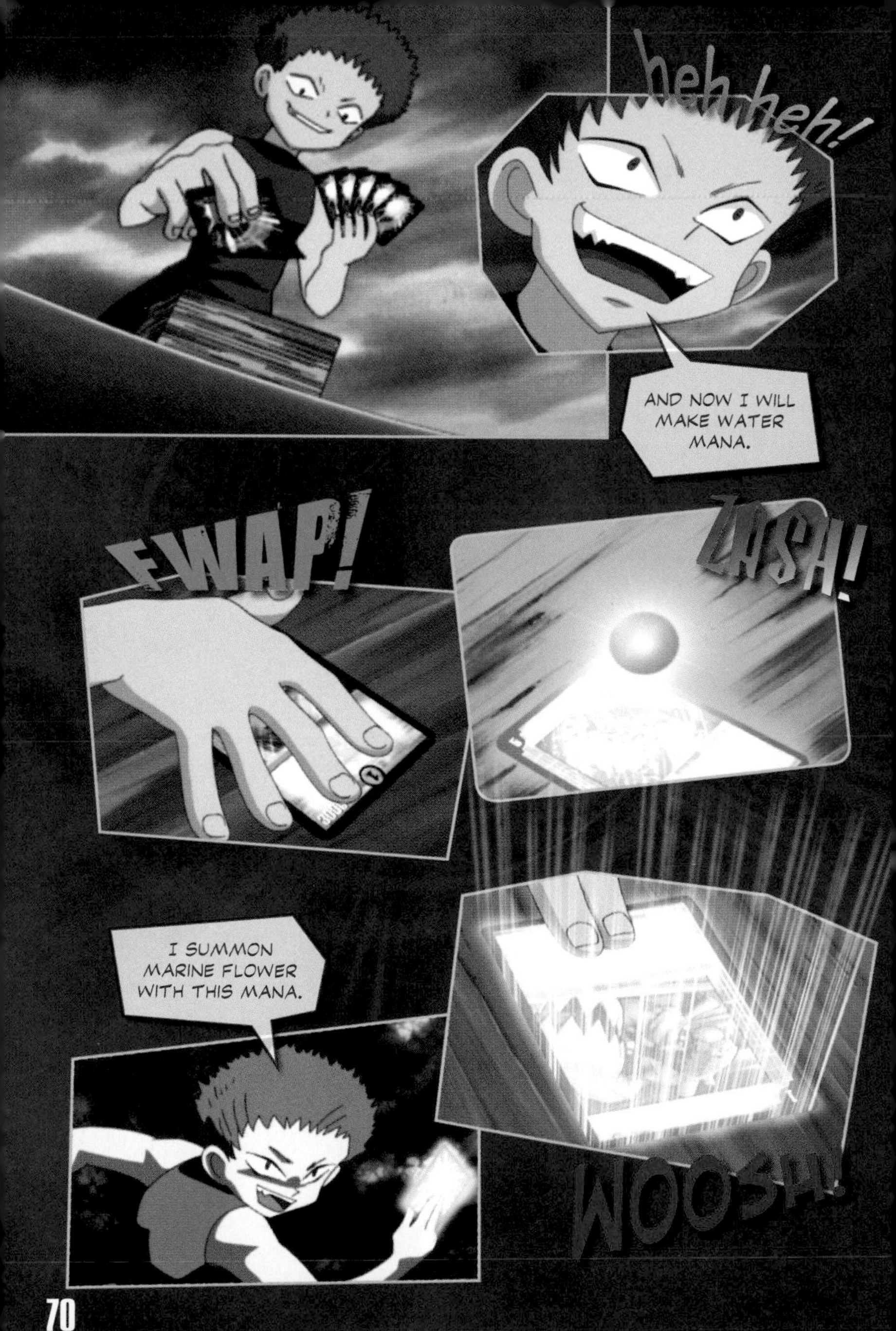
heh heh!
AND NOW I WILL MAKE WATER MANA.
FWAP!
ZASH!
I SUMMON MARINE FLOWER WITH THIS MANA.
WOOSH!

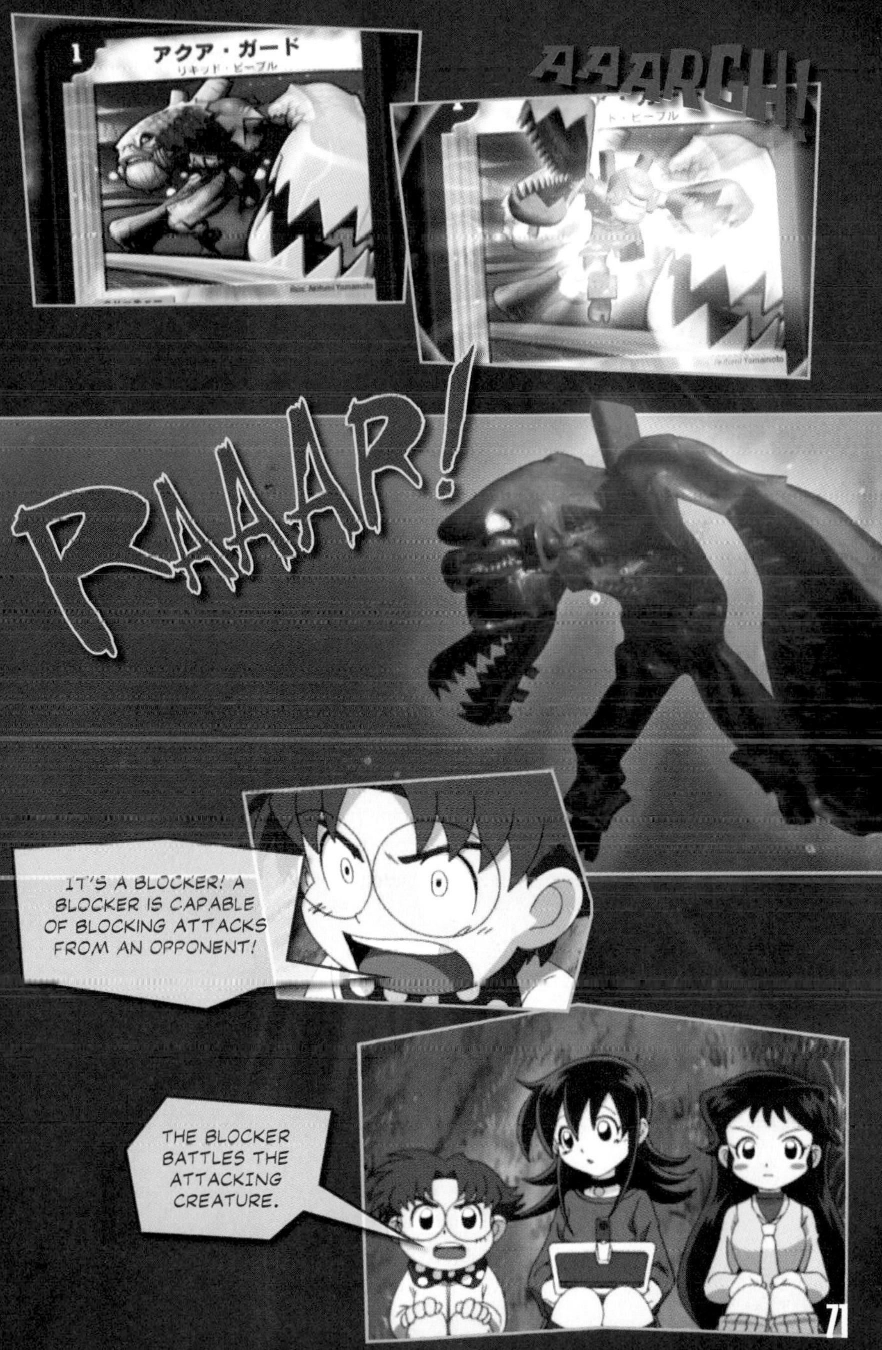
アクア・ガード
リキッド・ピープル
AAARGH!
RAAAR!
IT'S A BLOCKER! A BLOCKER IS CAPABLE OF BLOCKING ATTACKS FROM AN OPPONENT!
THE BLOCKER BATTLES THE ATTACKING CREATURE.

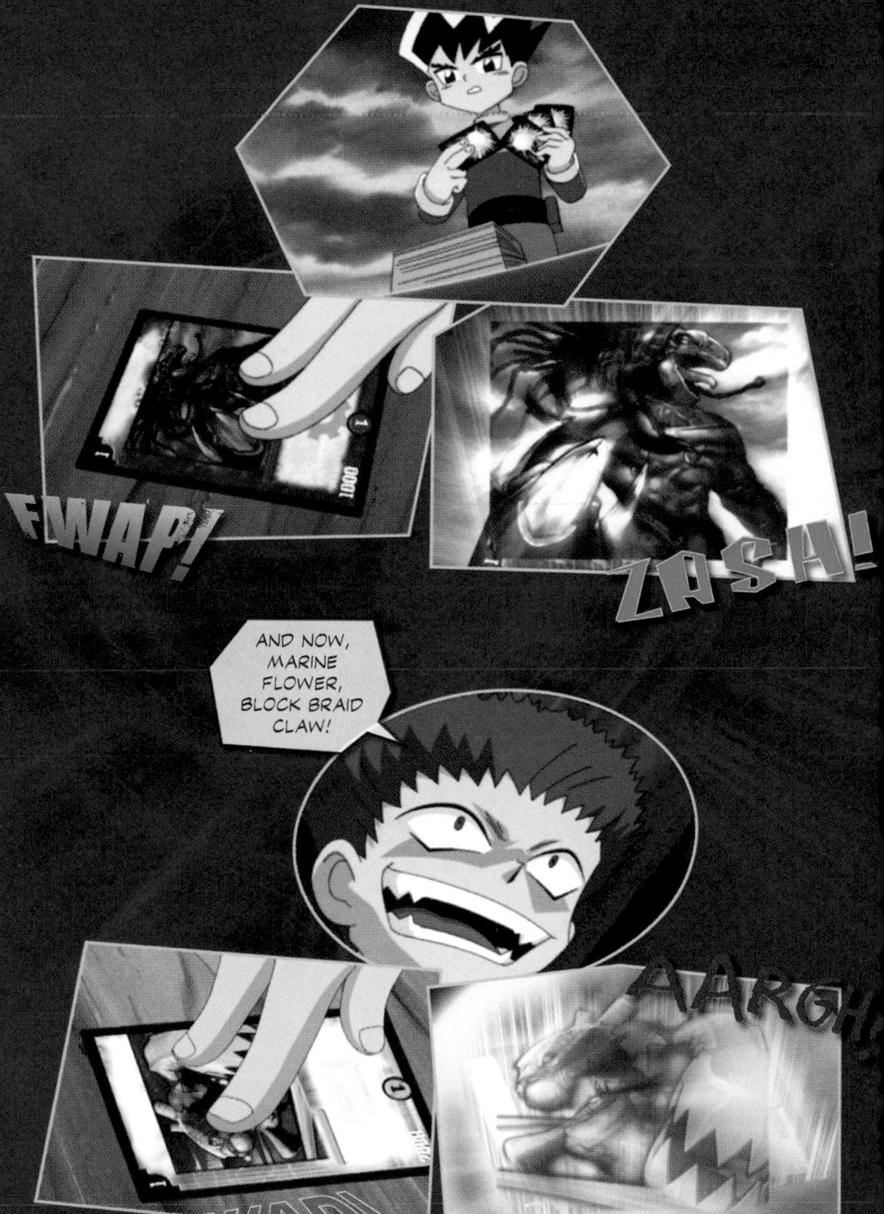

FWAP!
ZASH!
AND NOW, MARINE FLOWER, BLOCK BRAID CLAW!
AARGH!
FWAP!

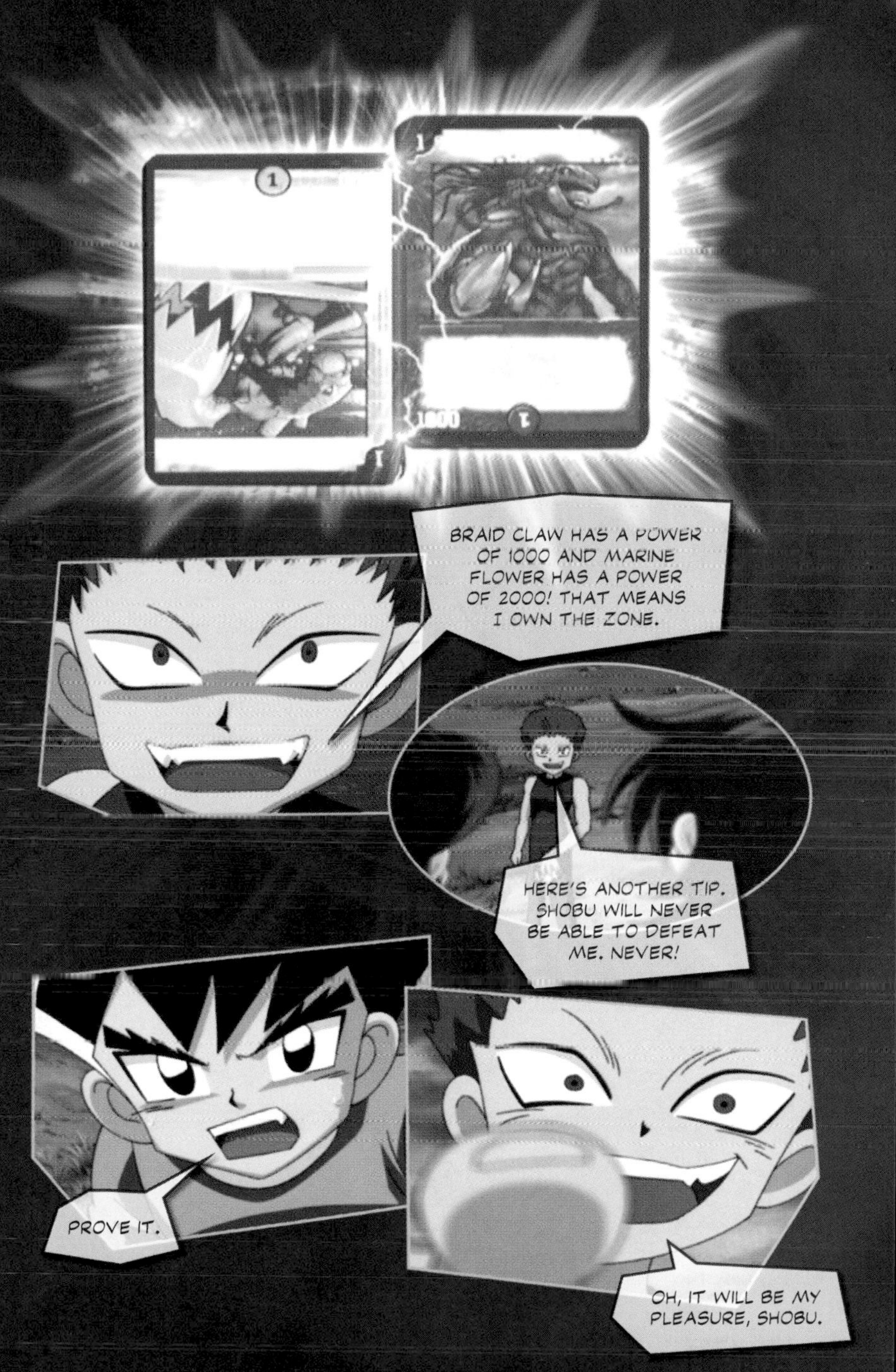
BRAID CLAW HAS A POWER OF 1000 AND MARINE FLOWER HAS A POWER OF 2000! THAT MEANS I OWN THE ZONE.
HERE'S ANOTHER TIP. SHOBU WILL NEVER BE ABLE TO DEFEAT ME. NEVER!
PROVE IT.
OH, IT WILL BE MY PLEASURE, SHOBU.

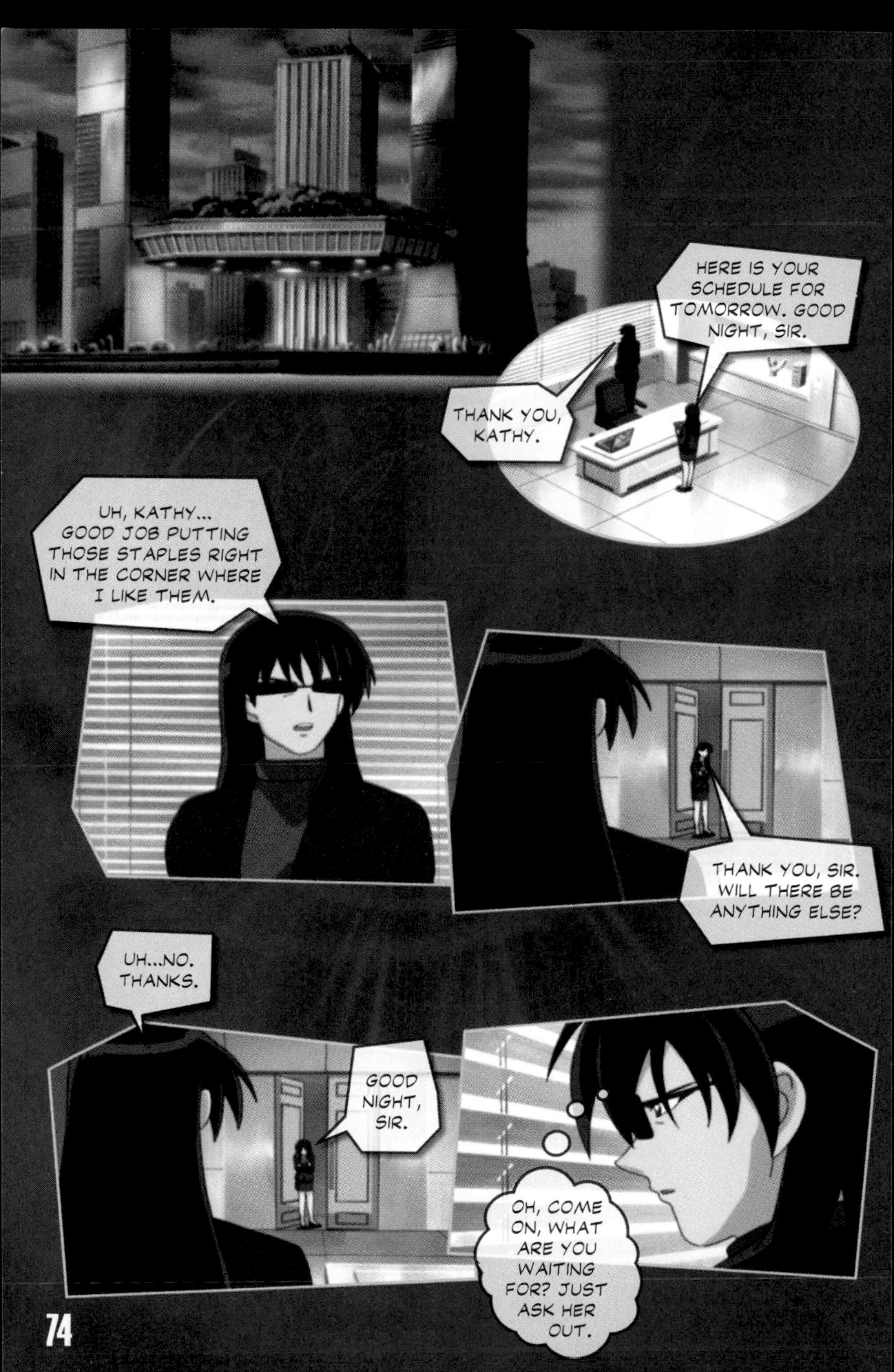
HERE IS YOUR SCHEDULE FOR TOMORROW. GOOD NIGHT, SIR.
THANK YOU, KATHY.
UH, KATHY... GOOD JOB PUTTING THOSE STAPLES RIGHT IN THE CORNER WHERE I LIKE THEM.
THANK YOU, SIR. WILL THERE BE ANYTHING ELSE?
UH...NO. THANKS.
GOOD NIGHT, SIR.
OH, COME ON, WHAT ARE YOU WAITING FOR? JUST ASK HER OUT.

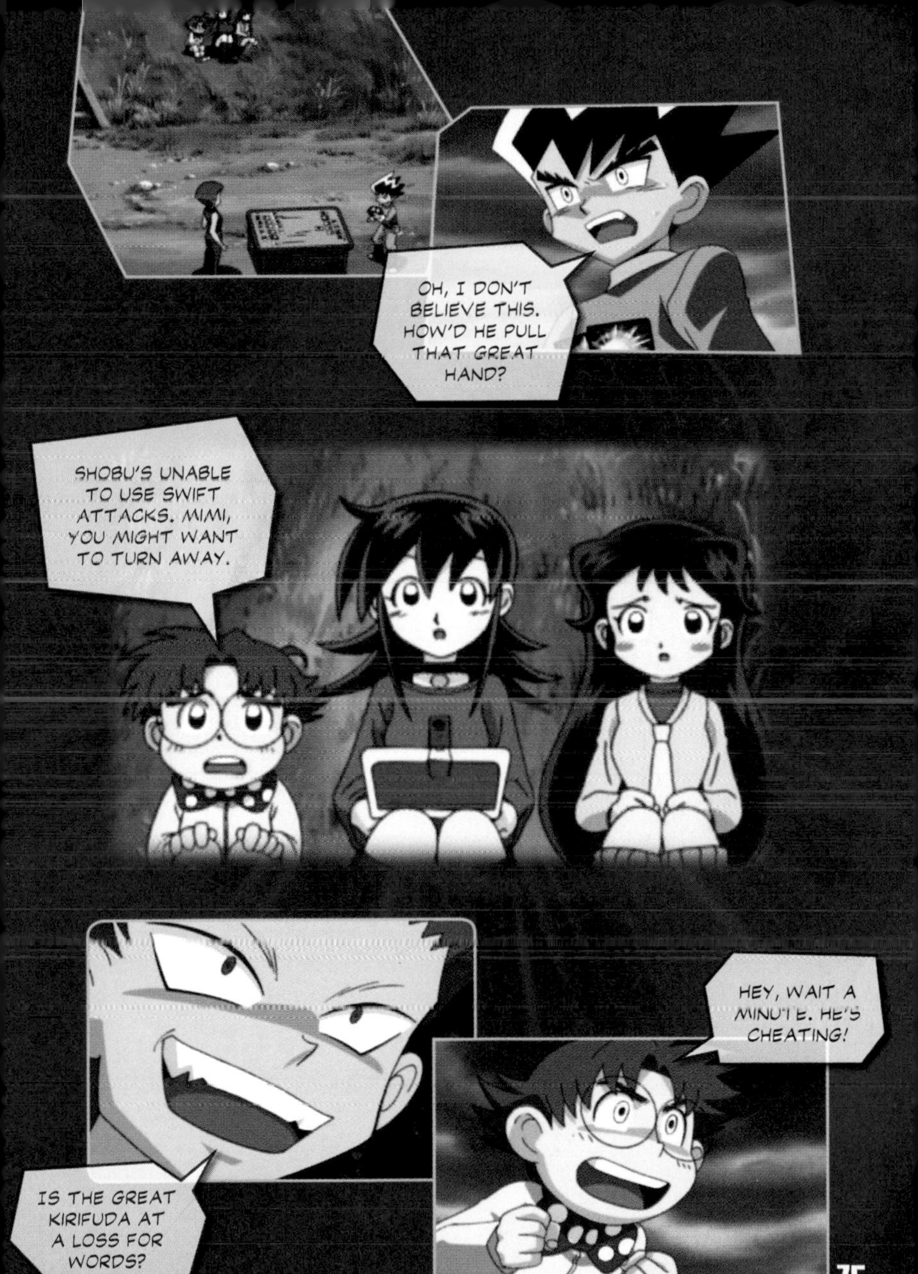

OH, I DON'T BELIEVE THIS. HOW'D HE PULL THAT GREAT HAND?
SHOBU'S UNABLE TO USE SWIFT ATTACKS. MIMI, YOU MIGHT WANT TO TURN AWAY.
HEY, WAIT A MINUTE. HE'S CHEATING!
IS THE GREAT KIRIFUDA AT A LOSS FOR WORDS?

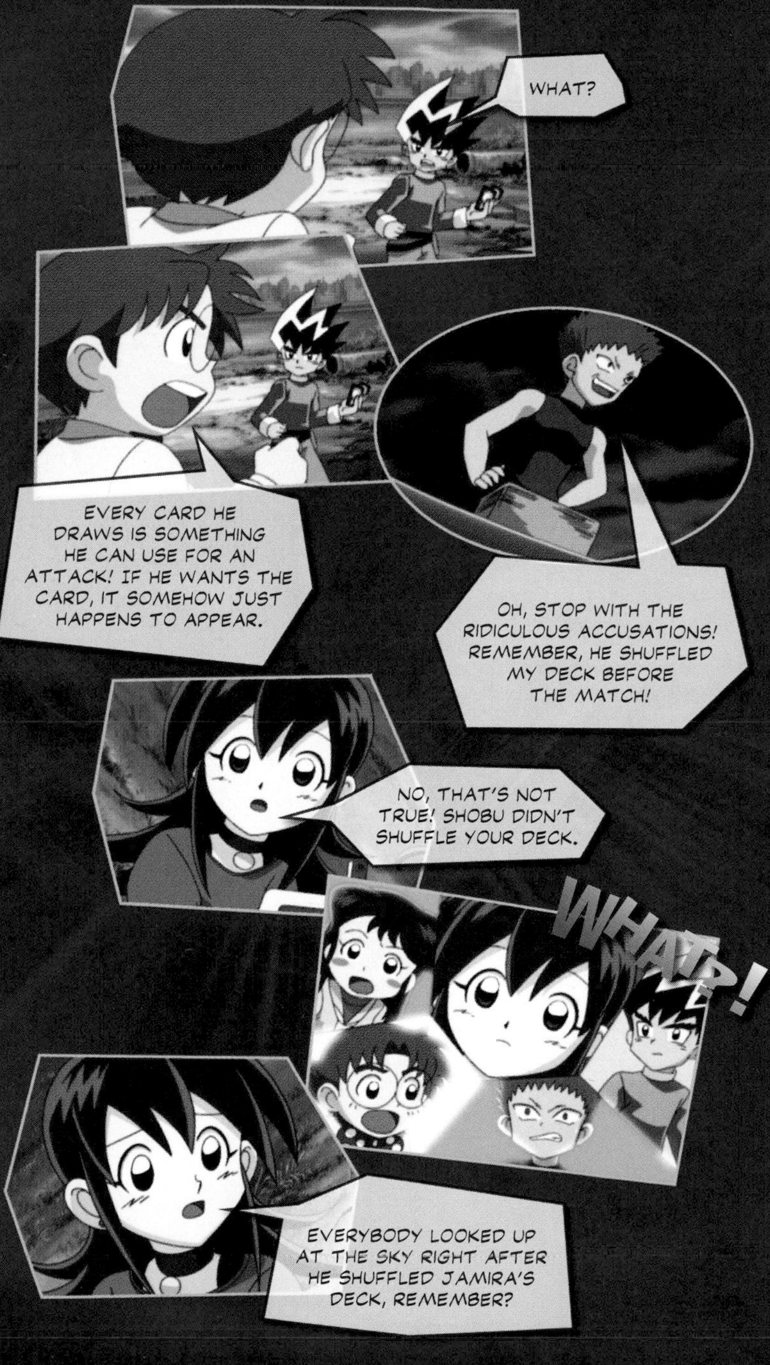
WHAT?
EVERY CARD HE DRAWS IS SOMETHING HE CAN USE FOR AN ATTACK! IF HE WANTS THE CARD, IT SOMEHOW JUST HAPPENS TO APPEAR.
OH, STOP WITH THE RIDICULOUS ACCUSATIONS! REMEMBER, HE SHUFFLED MY DECK BEFORE THE MATCH!
NO, THAT'S NOT TRUE! SHOBU DIDN'T SHUFFLE YOUR DECK.
WHAT?!
EVERYBODY LOOKED UP AT THE SKY RIGHT AFTER HE SHUFFLED JAMIRA'S DECK, REMEMBER?

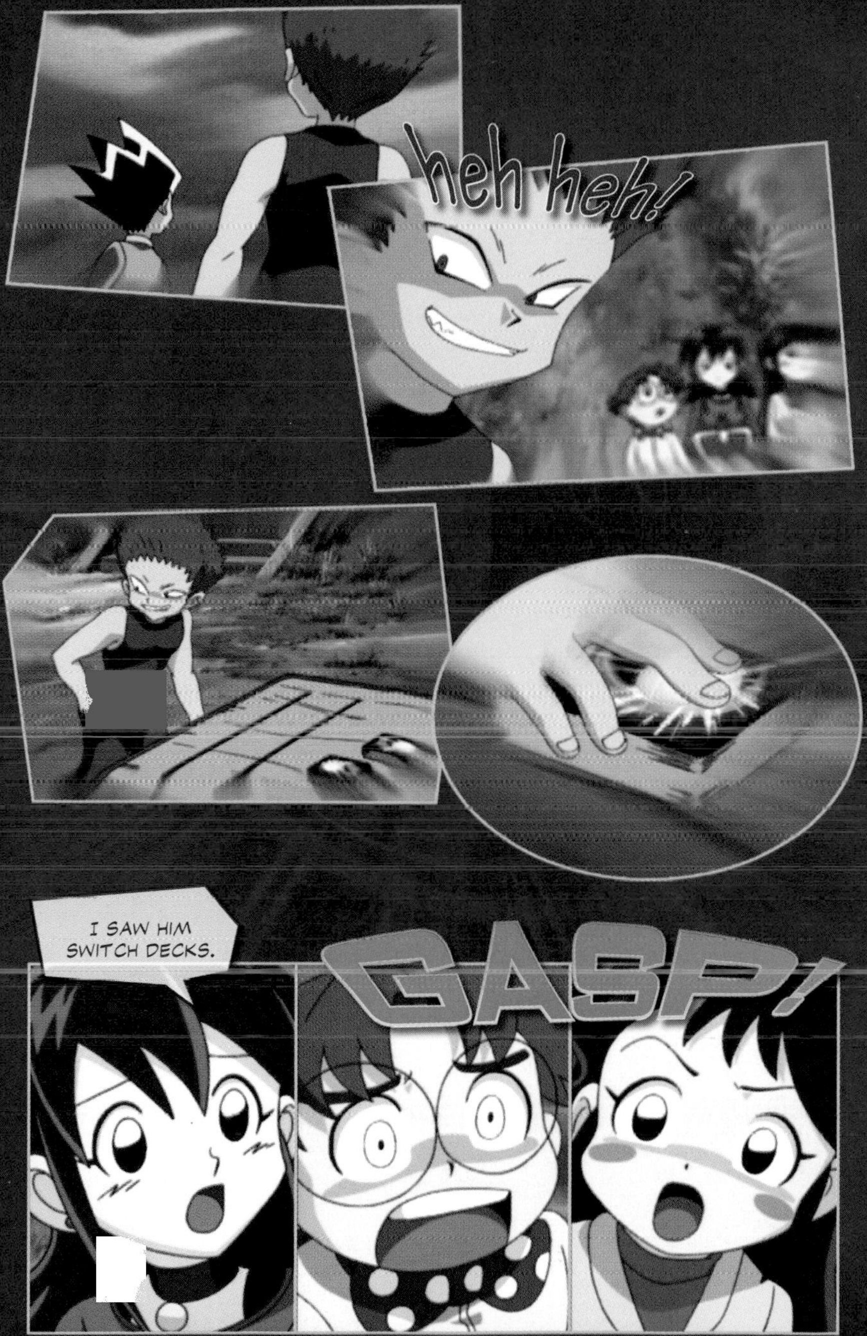
heh heh!
I SAW HIM SWITCH DECKS.
GASP!

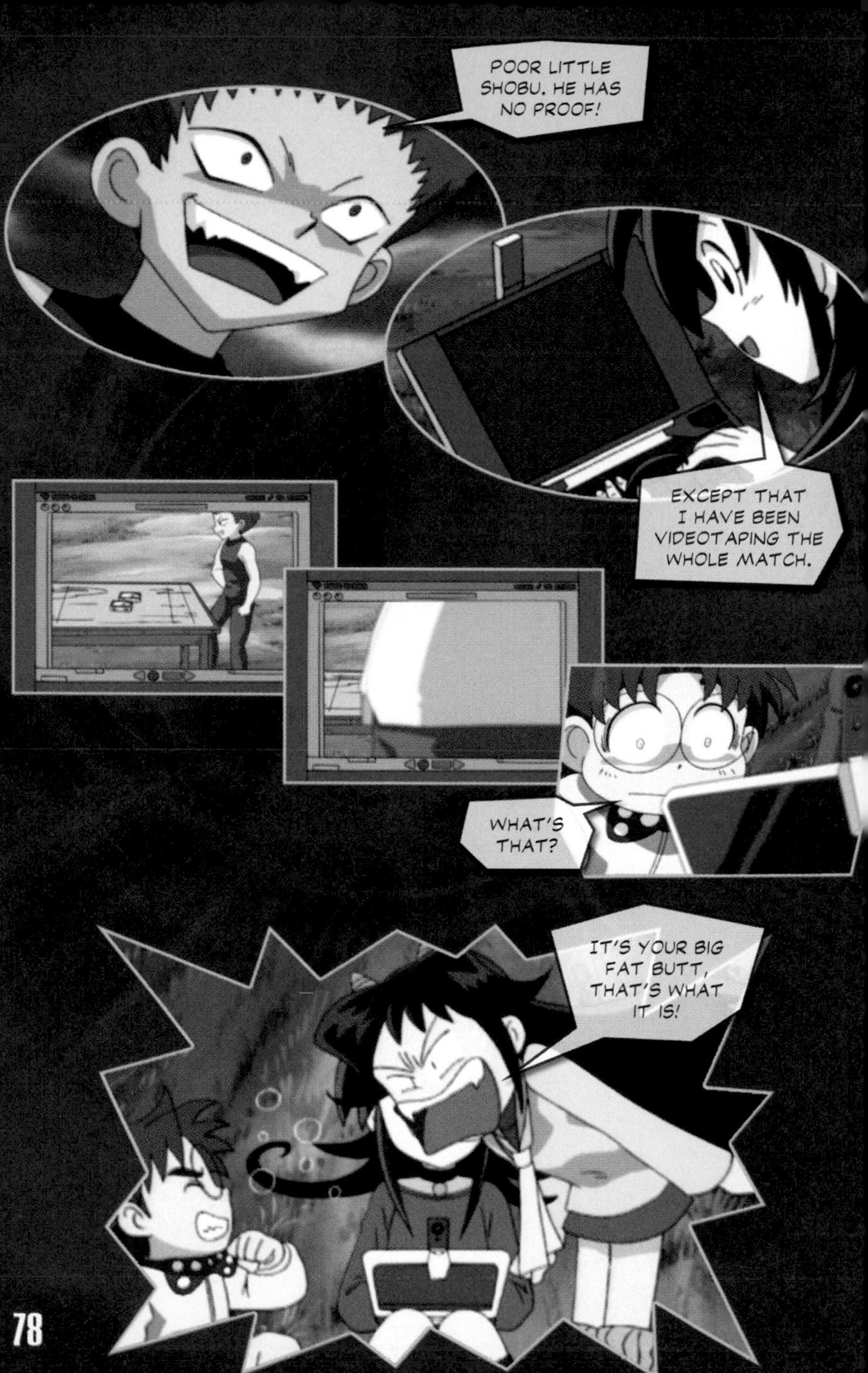

POOR LITTLE SHOBU. HE HAS NO PROOF!
EXCEPT THAT I HAVE BEEN VIDEOTAPING THE WHOLE MATCH.
WHAT'S THAT?
IT'S YOUR BIG FAT BUTT, THAT'S WHAT IT IS!

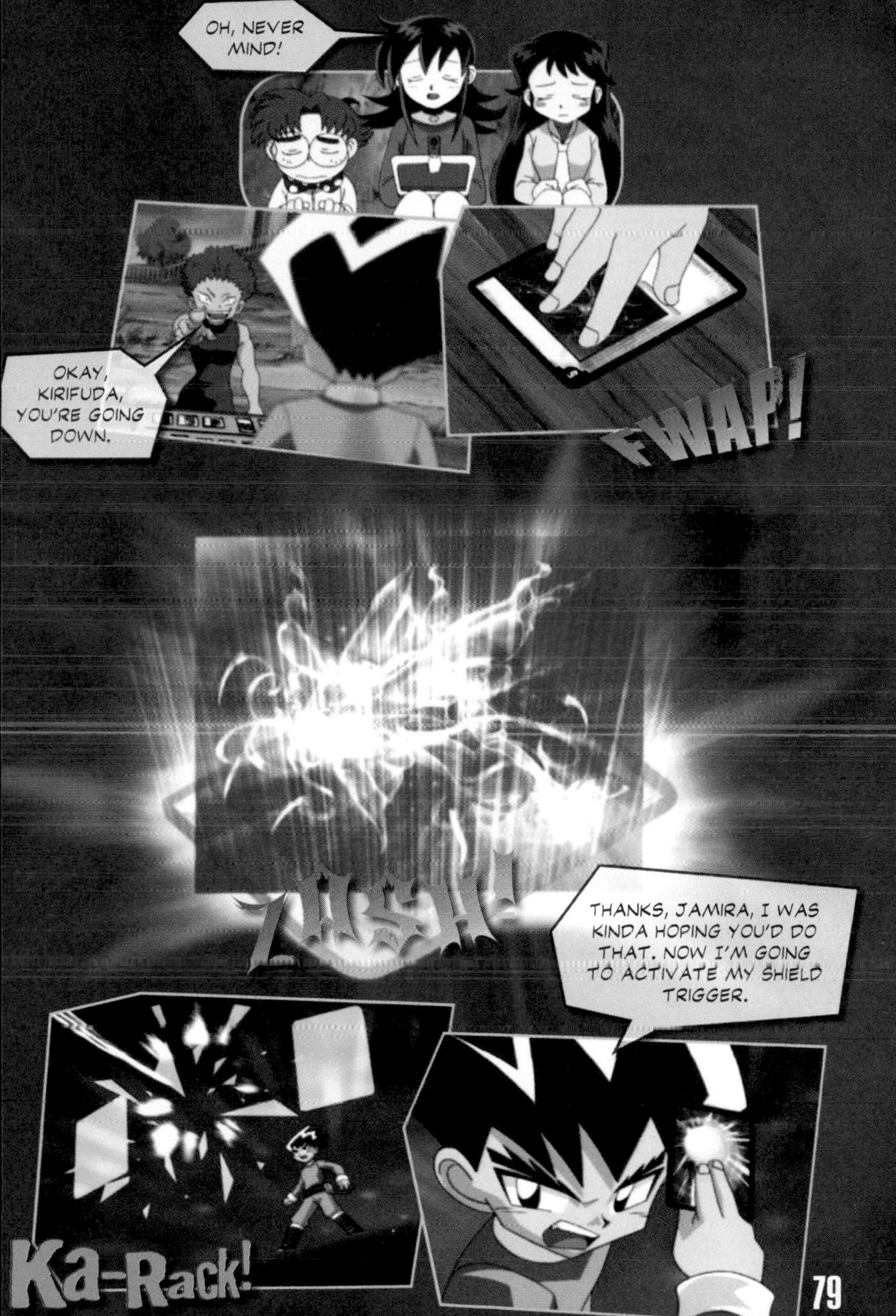
OH, NEVER MIND!
OKAY, KIRIFUDA, YOU'RE GOING DOWN.
FWAP!
THANKS, JAMIRA, I WAS KINDA HOPING YOU'D DO THAT. NOW I'M GOING TO ACTIVATE MY SHIELD TRIGGER.
Ka-Rack!

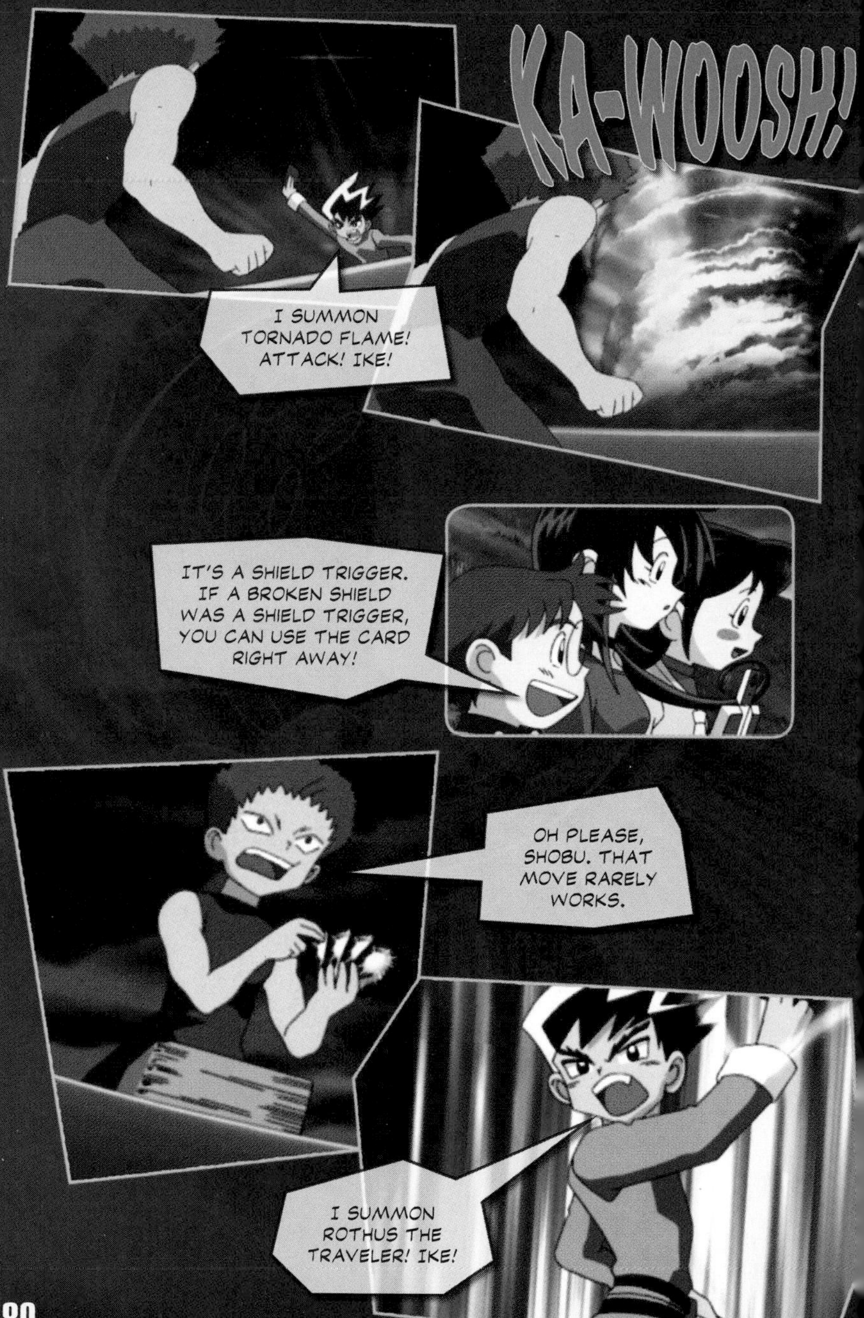
KA-WOOSH!
I SUMMON TORNADO FLAME! ATTACK! IKE!
IT'S A SHIELD TRIGGER. IF A BROKEN SHIELD WAS A SHIELD TRIGGER, YOU CAN USE THE CARD RIGHT AWAY!
OH PLEASE, SHOBU. THAT MOVE RARELY WORKS.
I SUMMON ROTHUS THE TRAVELER! IKE!

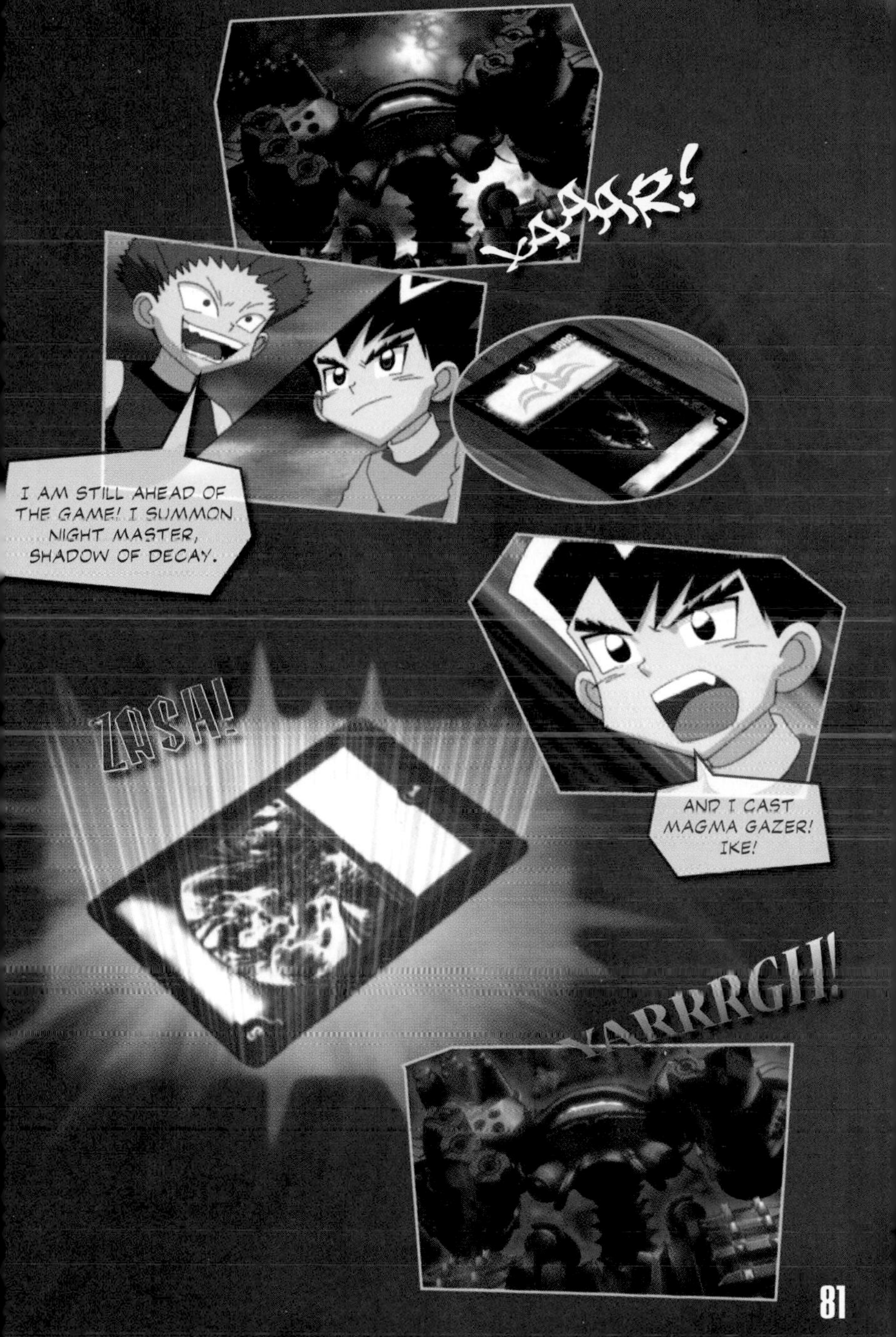
YAAAR!
I AM STILL AHEAD OF THE GAME! I SUMMON NIGHT MASTER, SHADOW OF DECAY.
AND I CAST MAGMA GAZER! IKE!
ZASH!
YARRRGH!

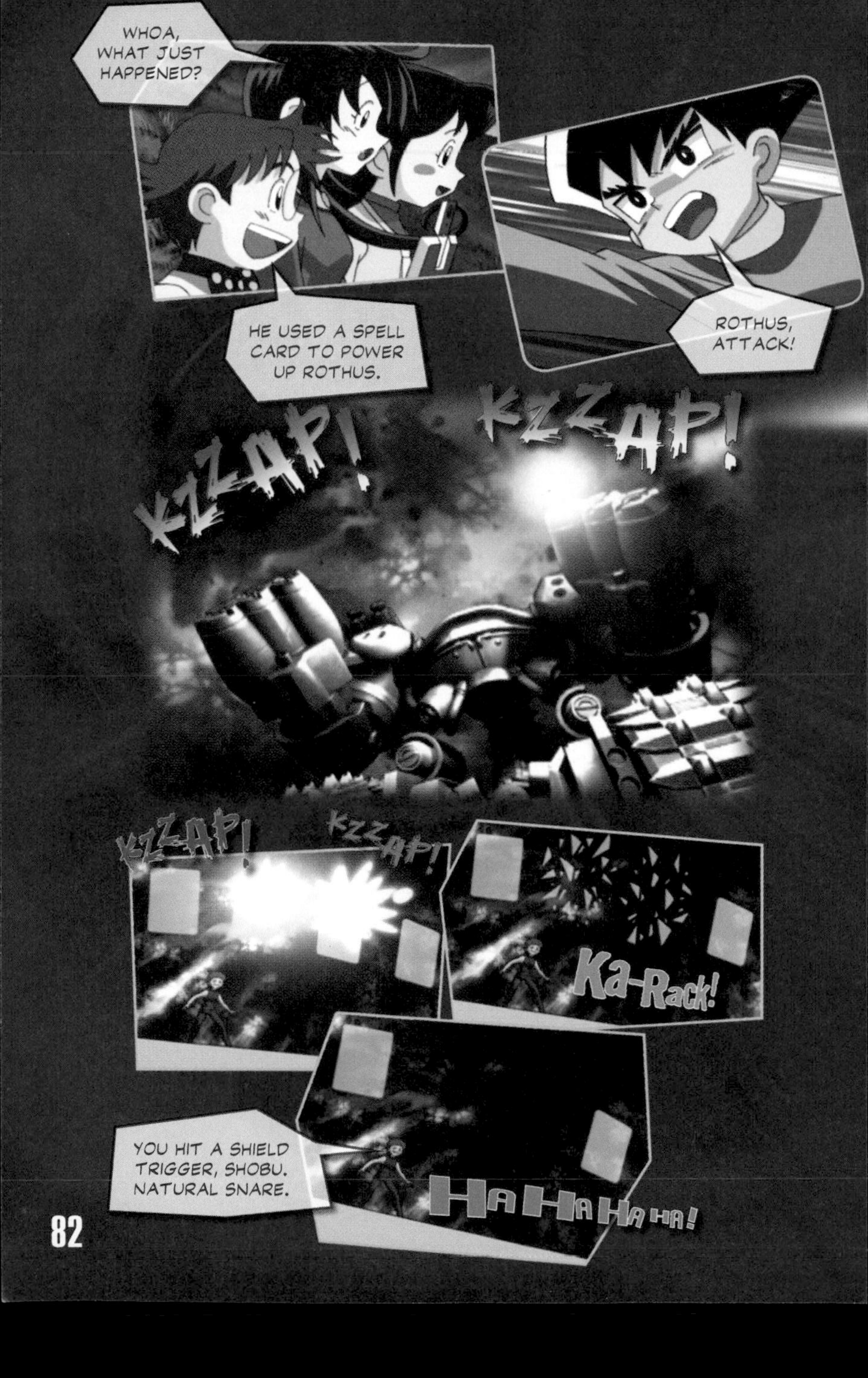
WHOA, WHAT JUST HAPPENED?
HE USED A SPELL CARD TO POWER UP ROTHUS.
ROTHUS, ATTACK!
KZZAP!
KZZAP!
KZZAP!
KZZAP!
Ka-Rack!
YOU HIT A SHIELD TRIGGER, SHOBU. NATURAL SNARE.
HaHaHaHaHa!

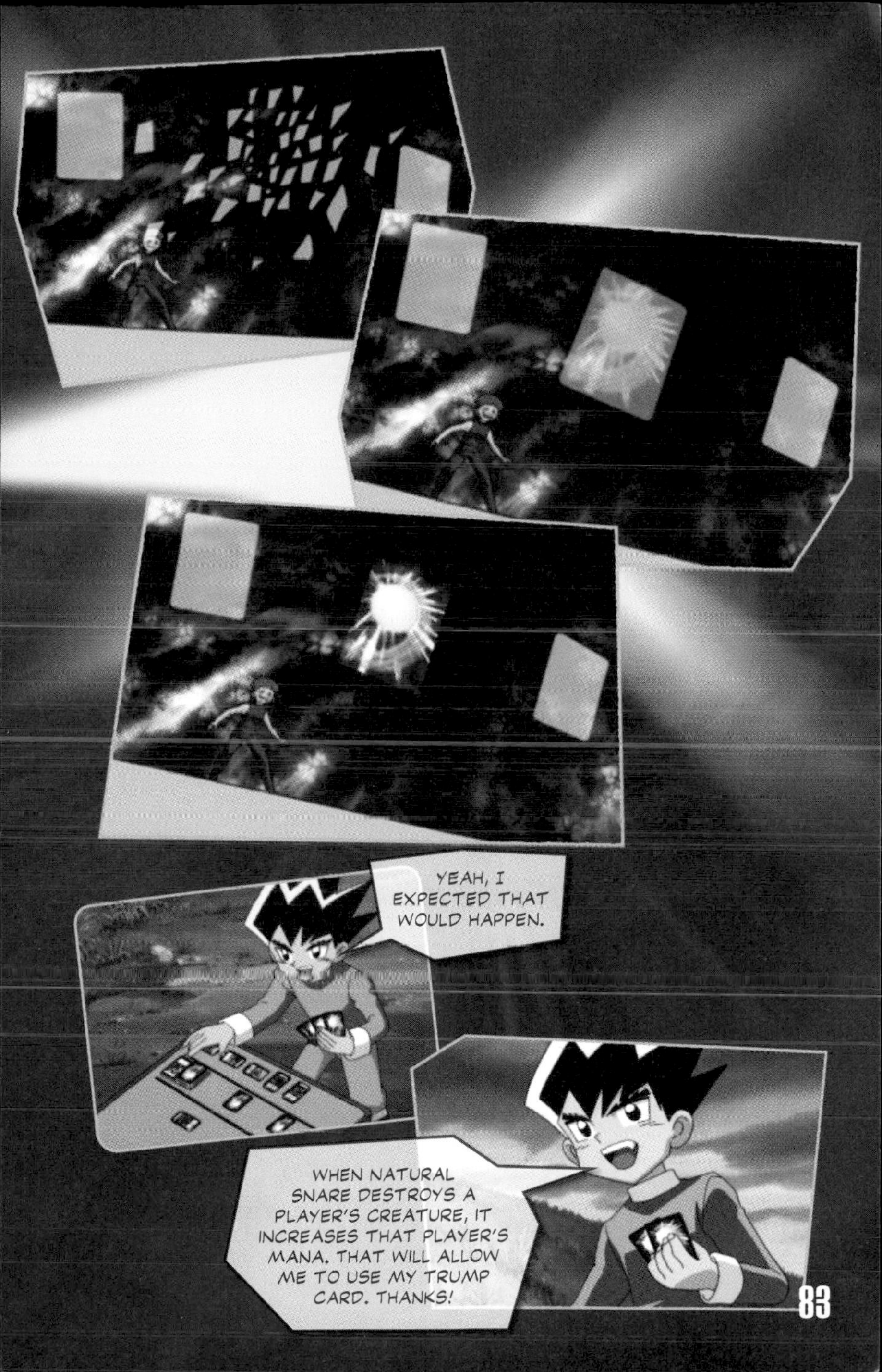
YEAH, I EXPECTED THAT WOULD HAPPEN.
WHEN NATURAL SNARE DESTROYS A PLAYER'S CREATURE, IT INCREASES THAT PLAYER'S MANA. THAT WILL ALLOW ME TO USE MY TRUMP CARD. THANKS!

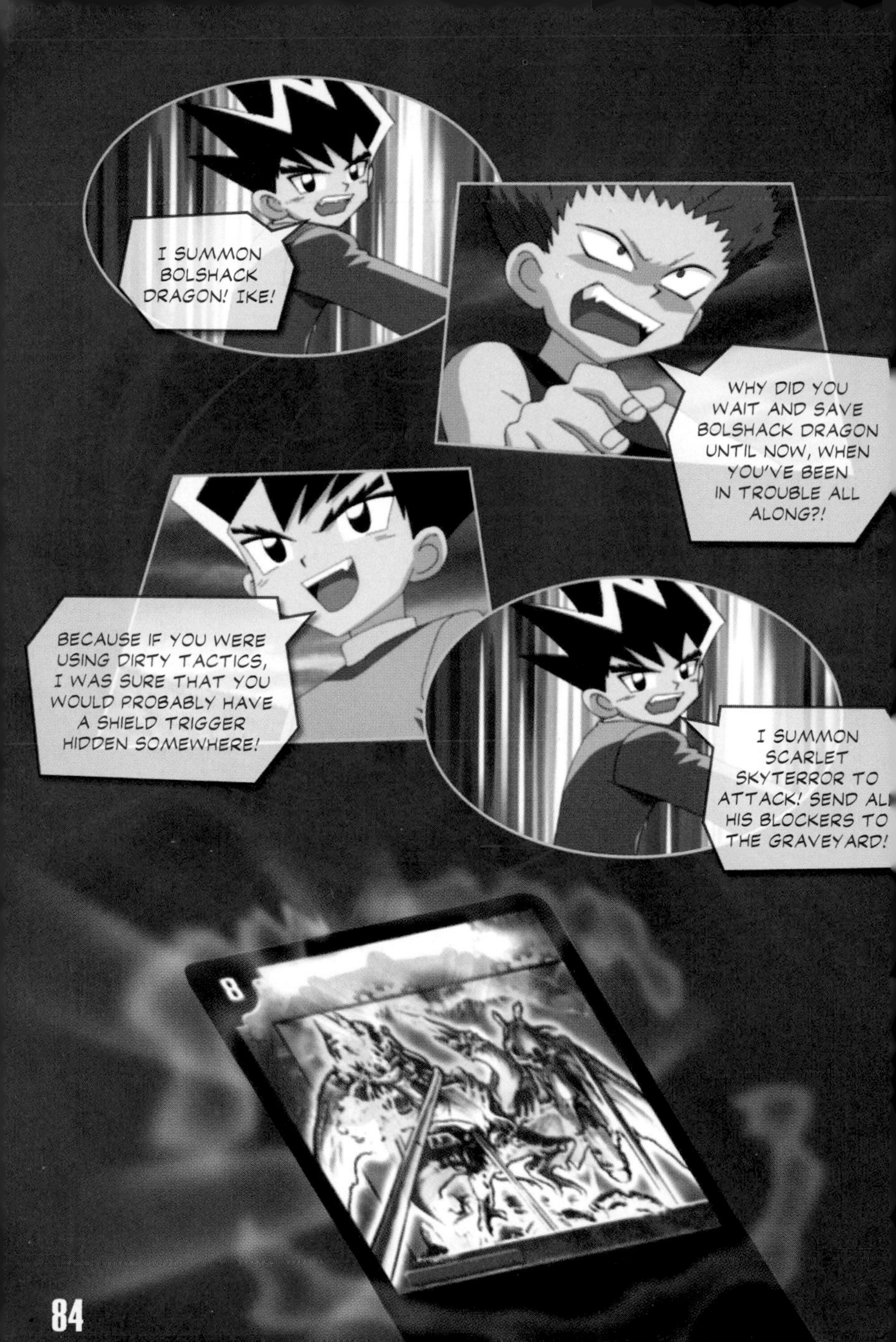
I SUMMON BOLSHACK DRAGON! IKE!
WHY DID YOU WAIT AND SAVE BOLSHACK DRAGON UNTIL NOW, WHEN YOU'VE BEEN IN TROUBLE ALL ALONG?!
BECAUSE IF YOU WERE USING DIRTY TACTICS, I WAS SURE THAT YOU WOULD PROBABLY HAVE A SHIELD TRIGGER HIDDEN SOMEWHERE!
I SUMMON SCARLET SKYTERROR TO ATTACK! SEND AL HIS BLOCKERS TO THE GRAVEYARD!
8

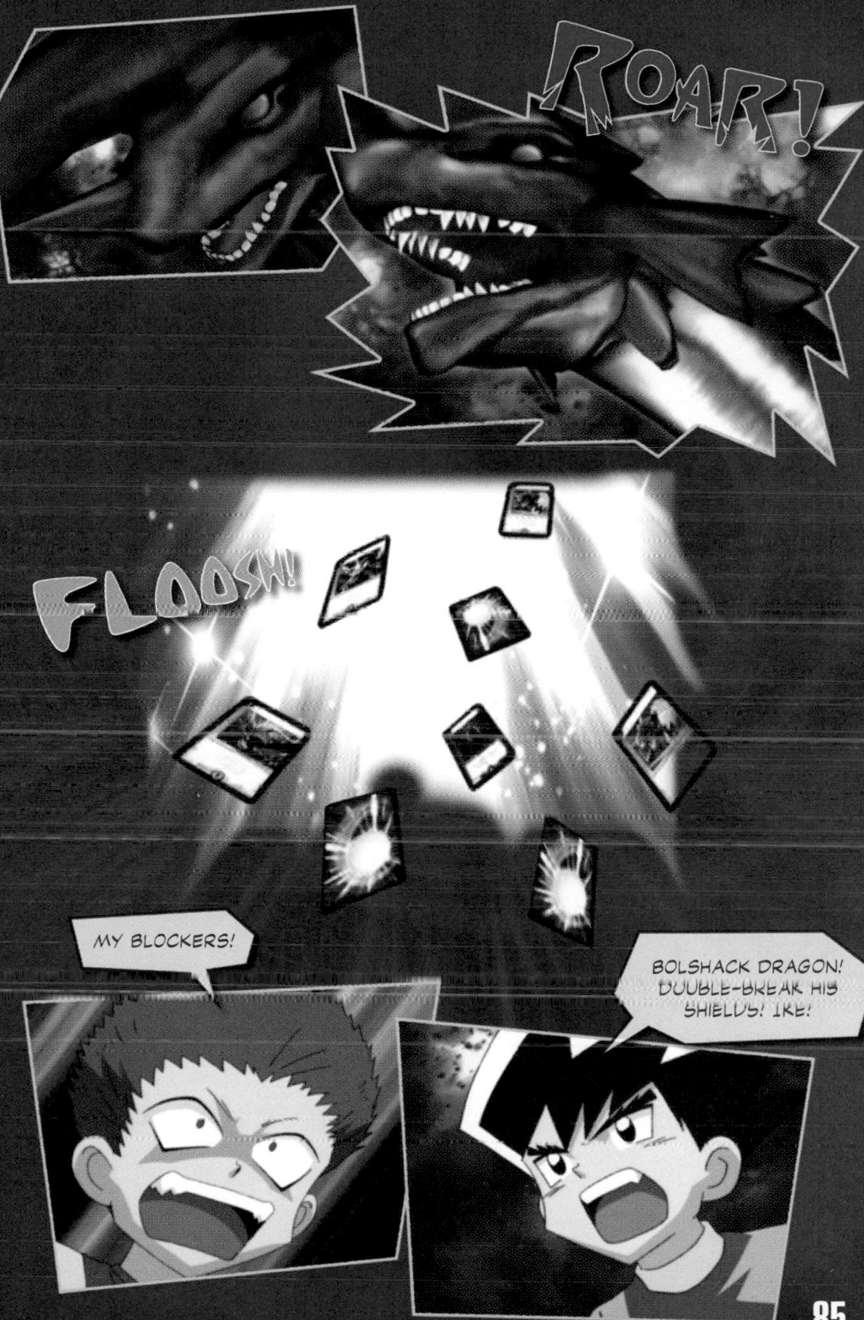
ROAR!
FLOOSH!
MY BLOCKERS!
BOLSHACK DRAGON! DOUBLE-BREAK HIS SHIELDS! IKE!

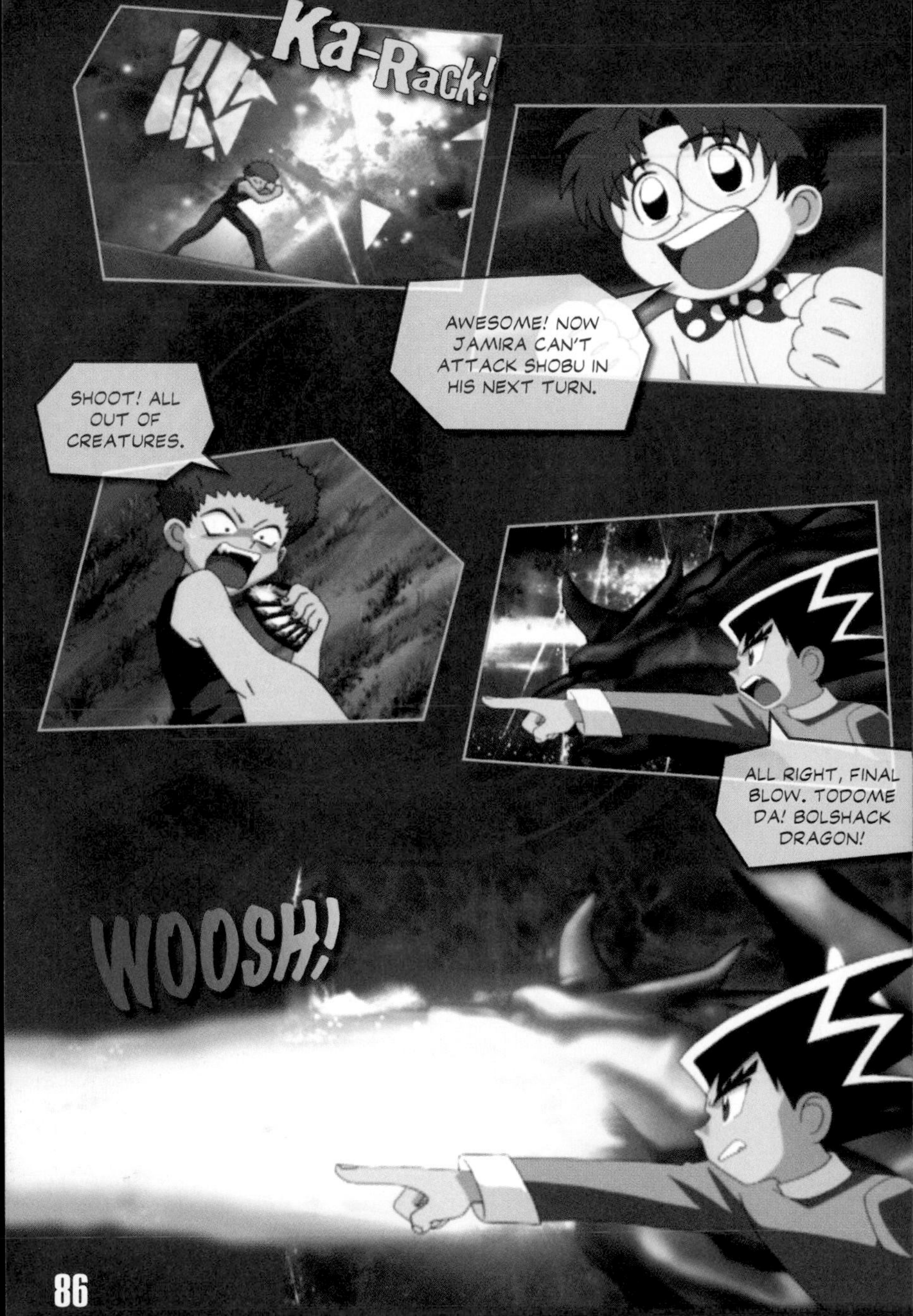

Ka-Rack!
AWESOME! NOW JAMIRA CAN'T ATTACK SHOBU IN HIS NEXT TURN.
SHOOT! ALL OUT OF CREATURES.
ALL RIGHT, FINAL BLOW. TODOME DA! BOLSHACK DRAGON!
WOOSH!

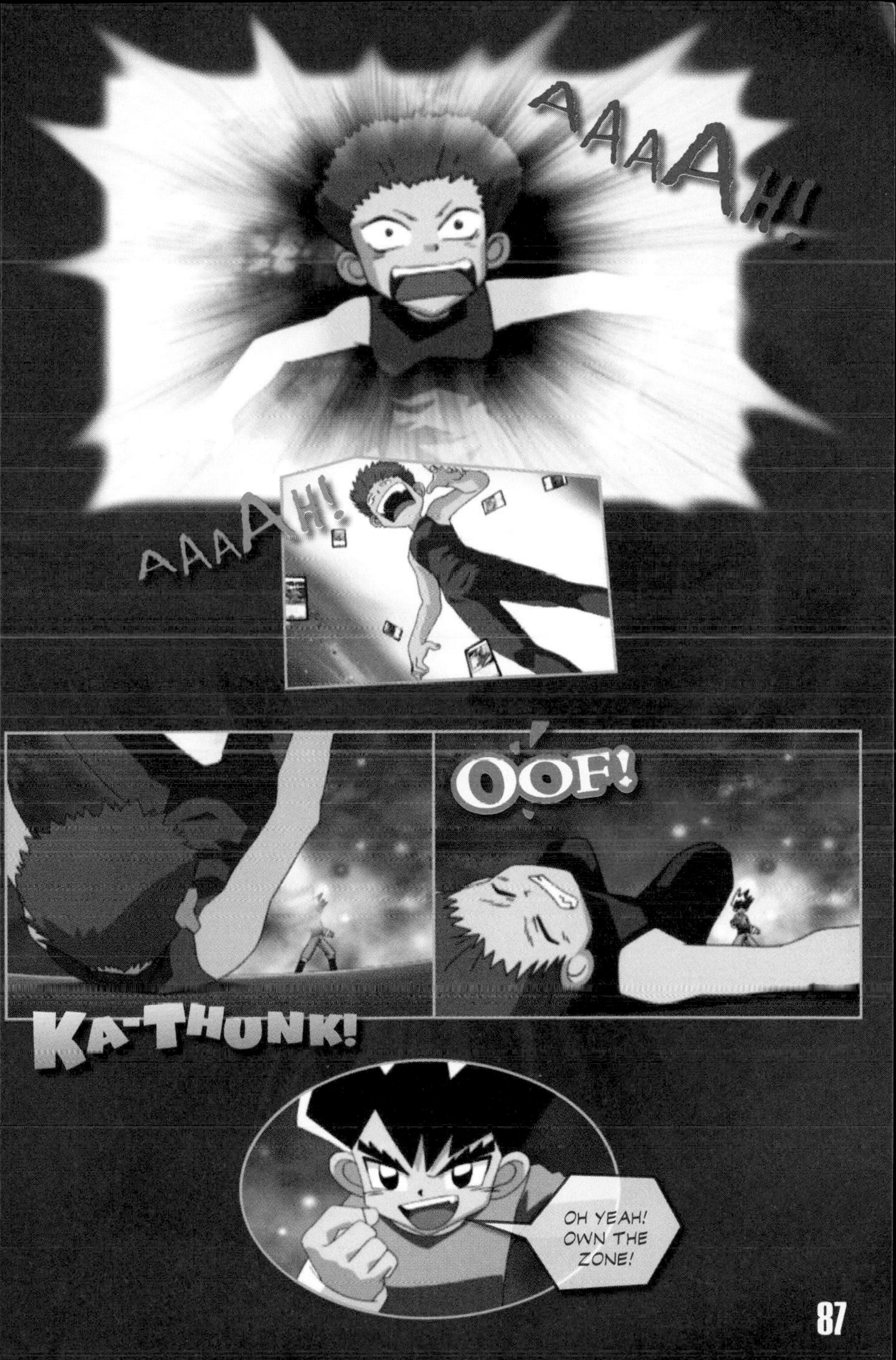
AAAAAH!!
AAAAH!
OOF!
KA-THUNK!
OH YEAH! OWN THE ZONE!

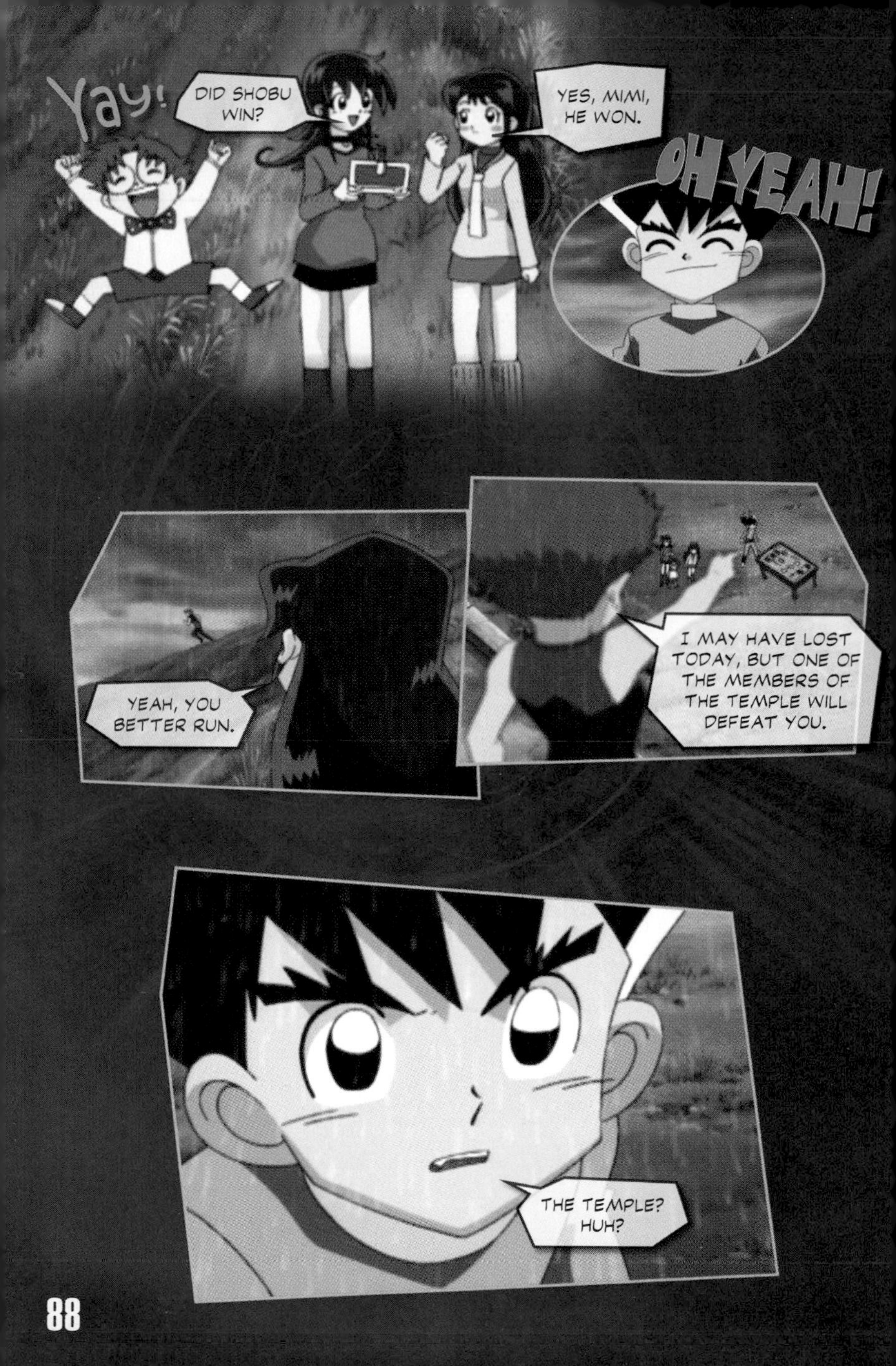

Yay!
DID SHOBU WIN?
YES, MIMI, HE WON.
OH YEAH!
YEAH, YOU BETTER RUN.
I MAY HAVE LOST TODAY, BUT ONE OF THE MEMBERS OF THE TEMPLE WILL DEFEAT YOU.
THE TEMPLE? HUH?

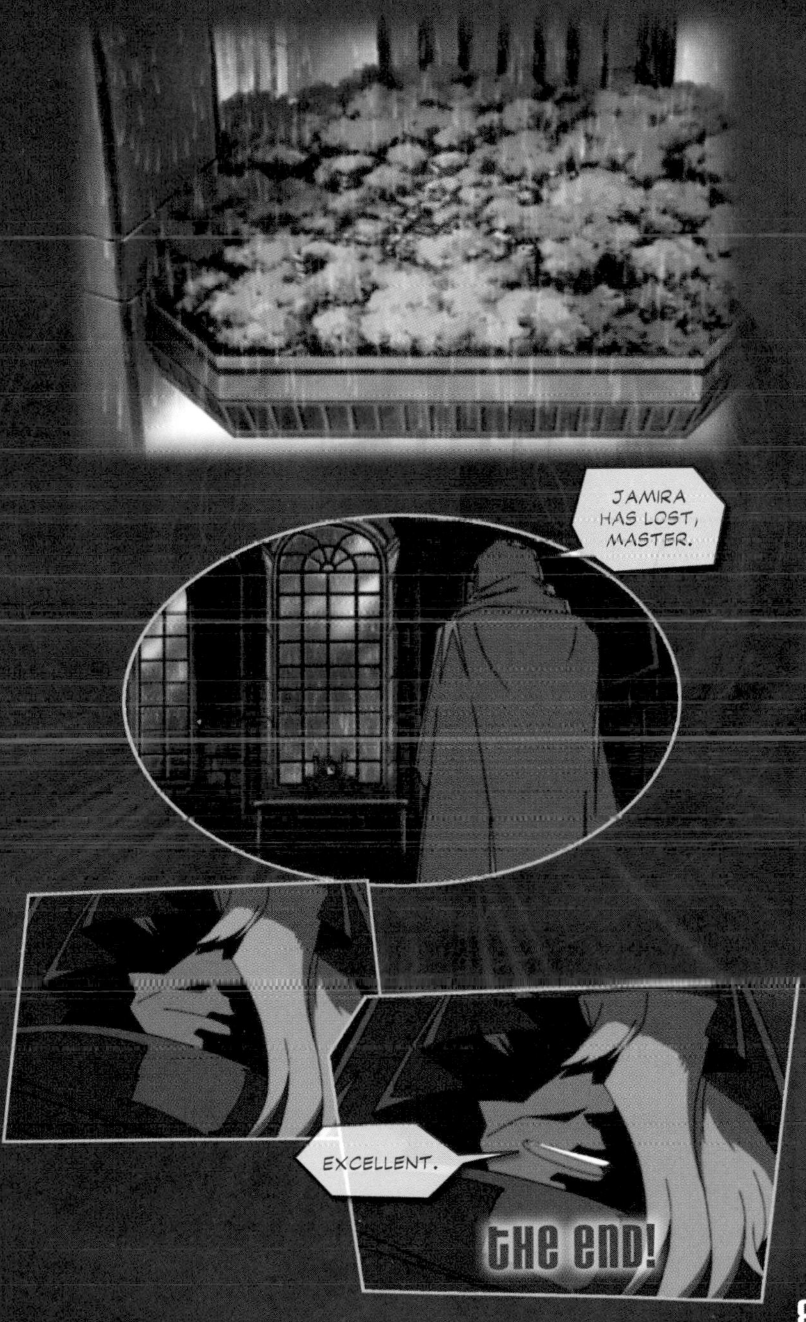
JAMIRA HAS LOST, MASTER.
EXCELLENT.
THE END!

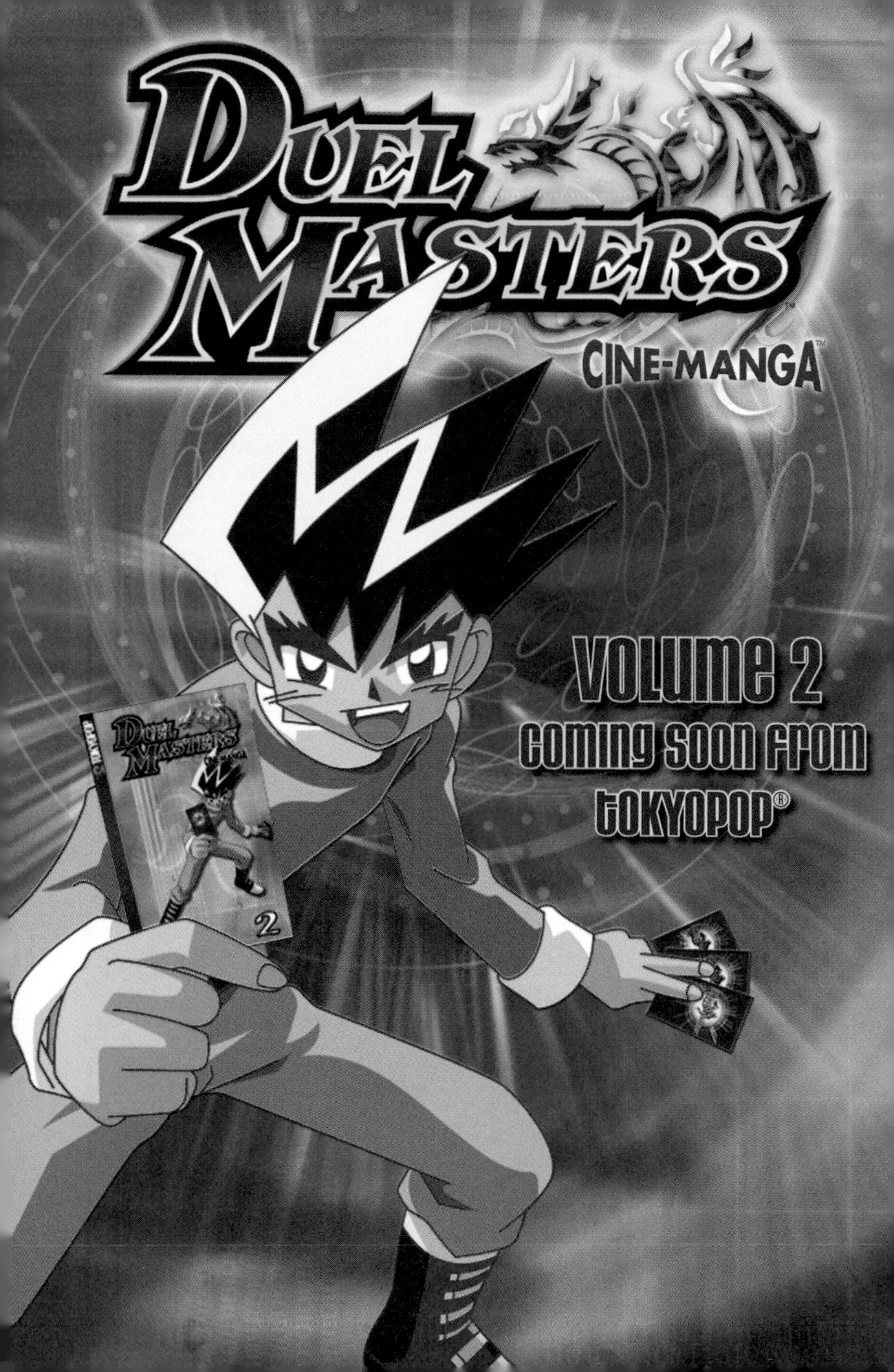

DUEL MASTERS™
CINE-MANGA™
VOLUME 2
COMING SOON FROM
TOKYOPOP®

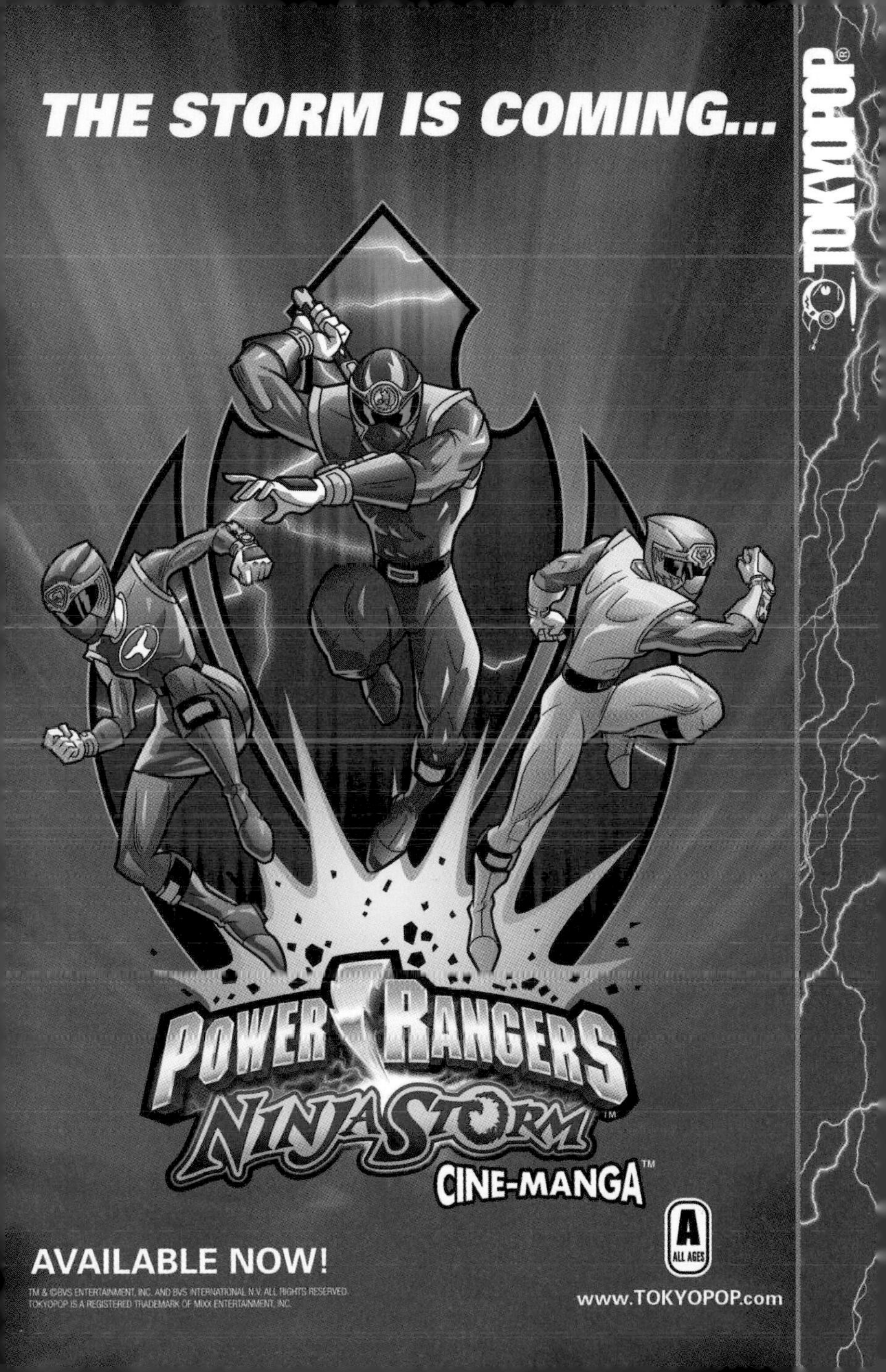

THE STORM IS COMING...

TOKYOPOP®

POWER RANGERS
NINJA STORM ™
CINE-MANGA ™

AVAILABLE NOW!

TM & ©BVS ENTERTAINMENT, INC. AND BVS INTERNATIONAL, N.V. ALL RIGHTS RESERVED.
TOKYOPOP IS A REGISTERED TRADEMARK OF MIXX ENTERTAINMENT, INC.

ALL AGES

www.TOKYOPOP.com

ALSO AVAILABLE FROM TOKYOPOP

MANGA

.HACK//LEGEND OF THE TWILIGHT
ANGELIC LAYER
BABY BIRTH
BRAIN POWERED
BRIGADOON
B'TX
CANDIDATE FOR GODDESS, THE
CARDCAPTOR SAKURA
CARDCAPTOR SAKURA - MASTER OF THE CLOW
CHRONICLES OF THE CURSED SWORD
CLAMP SCHOOL DETECTIVES
CLOVER
COMIC PARTY
CORRECTOR YUI
COWBOY BEBOP
COWBOY BEBOP: SHOOTING STAR
CRAZY LOVE STORY
CRESCENT MOON
CULDCEPT
CYBORG 009
D•N•ANGEL
DEMON DIARY
DEMON OROON, THE
DIGIMON
DIGIMON TAMERS
DIGIMON ZERO TWO
DRAGON HUNTER
DRAGON KNIGHTS
DRAGON VOICE
DREAM SAGA
DUKLYON: CLAMP SCHOOL DEFENDERS
ET CETERA
ETERNITY
FAERIES' LANDING
FLCL
FORBIDDEN DANCE
FRUITS BASKET
G GUNDAM
GATEKEEPERS
GIRL GOT GAME
GUNDAM BLUE DESTINY
GUNDAM SEED ASTRAY
GUNDAM WING
GUNDAM WING: BATTLEFIELD OF PACIFISTS
GUNDAM WING: ENDLESS WALTZ

GUNDAM WING: THE LAST OUTPOST (G-UNIT)
HANDS OFF!
HARLEM BEAT
IMMORTAL RAIN
I.N.V.U.
INITIAL D
INSTANT TEEN: JUST ADD NUTS
JING: KING OF BANDITS
JING: KING OF BANDITS - TWILIGHT TALES
JULINE
KARE KANO
KILL ME, KISS ME
KINDAICHI CASE FILES, THE
KING OF HELL
KODOCHA: SANA'S STAGE
LEGEND OF CHUN HYANG, THE
MAGIC KNIGHT RAYEARTH I
MAGIC KNIGHT RAYEARTH II
MAN OF MANY FACES
MARMALADE BOY
MARS
MARS: HORSE WITH NO NAME
METROID
MINK
MIRACLE GIRLS
MODEL
ONE
ONE I LOVE, THE
PEACH GIRL
PEACH GIRL: CHANGE OF HEART
PITA-TEN
PLANET LADDER
PLANETES
PRINCESS AI
PSYCHIC ACADEMY
RAGNAROK
RAVE MASTER
REALITY CHECK
REBIRTH
REBOUND
RISING STARS OF MANGA
SAILOR MOON
SAINT TAIL
SAMURAI GIRL REAL BOUT HIGH SCHOOL
SEIKAI TRILOGY, THE
SGT. FROG
SHAOLIN SISTERS

ALSO AVAILABLE FROM 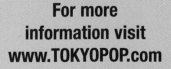 TOKYOPOP®

**For more
information visit
www.TOKYOPOP.com**

03.03.04Y

TOKYOPOP®

JACKIE CHAN

ADVENTURES

Cine-Manga™ based on the hit show on Kids' WB!™

成龍歷險

www.TOKYOPOP.com

TM & © 2003 Adelaide Productions, Inc. All Rights Reserved. Kids' WB! TM & © Warner Bros. 2003

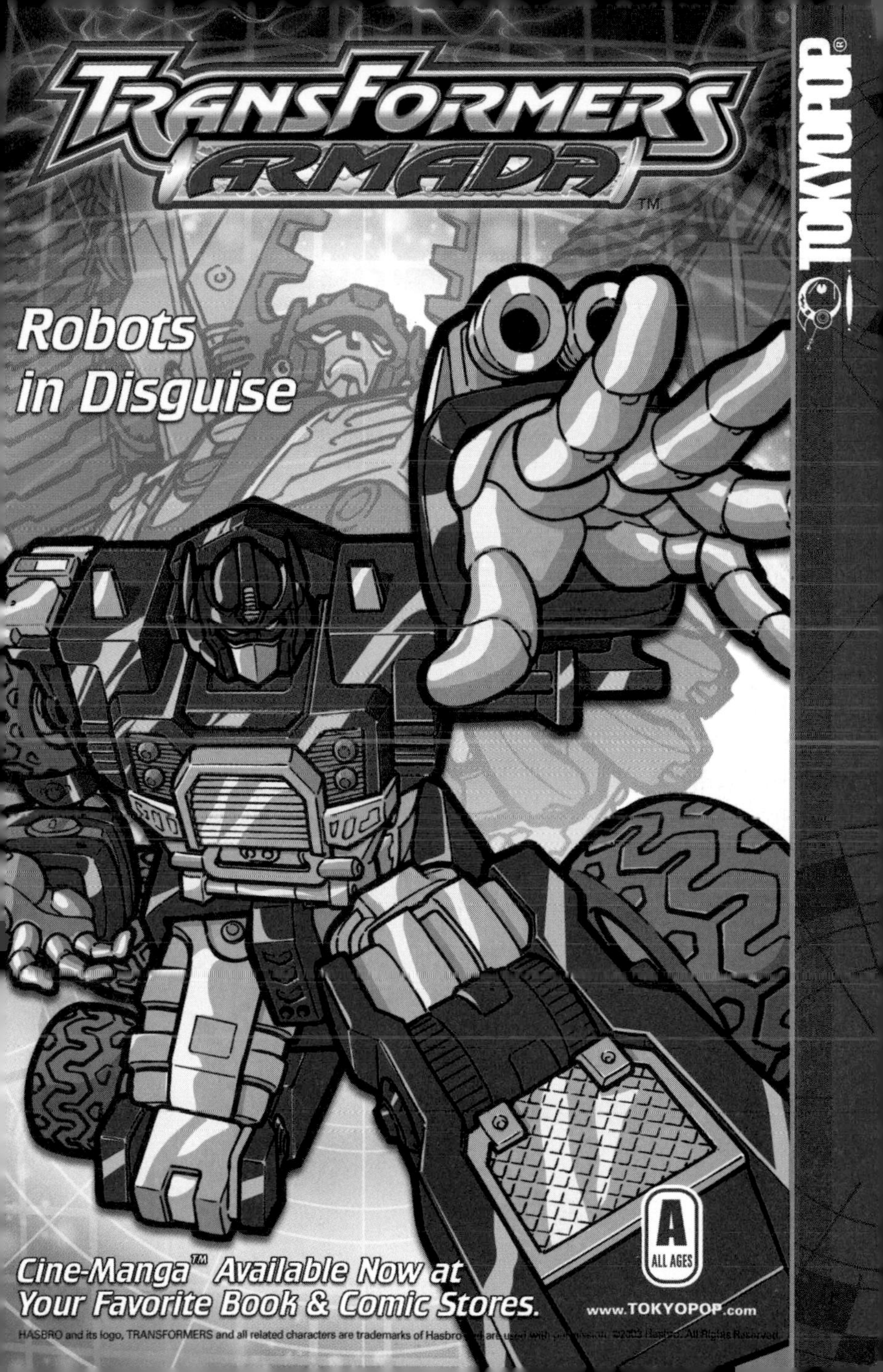
TRANSFORMERS ARMADA™
TOKYOPOP®
Robots in Disguise
A ALL AGES
Cine-Manga™ Available Now at Your Favorite Book & Comic Stores.
www.TOKYOPOP.com
HASBRO and its logo, TRANSFORMERS and all related characters are trademarks of Hasbro and are used with permission. ©2003 Hasbro. All Rights Reserved.

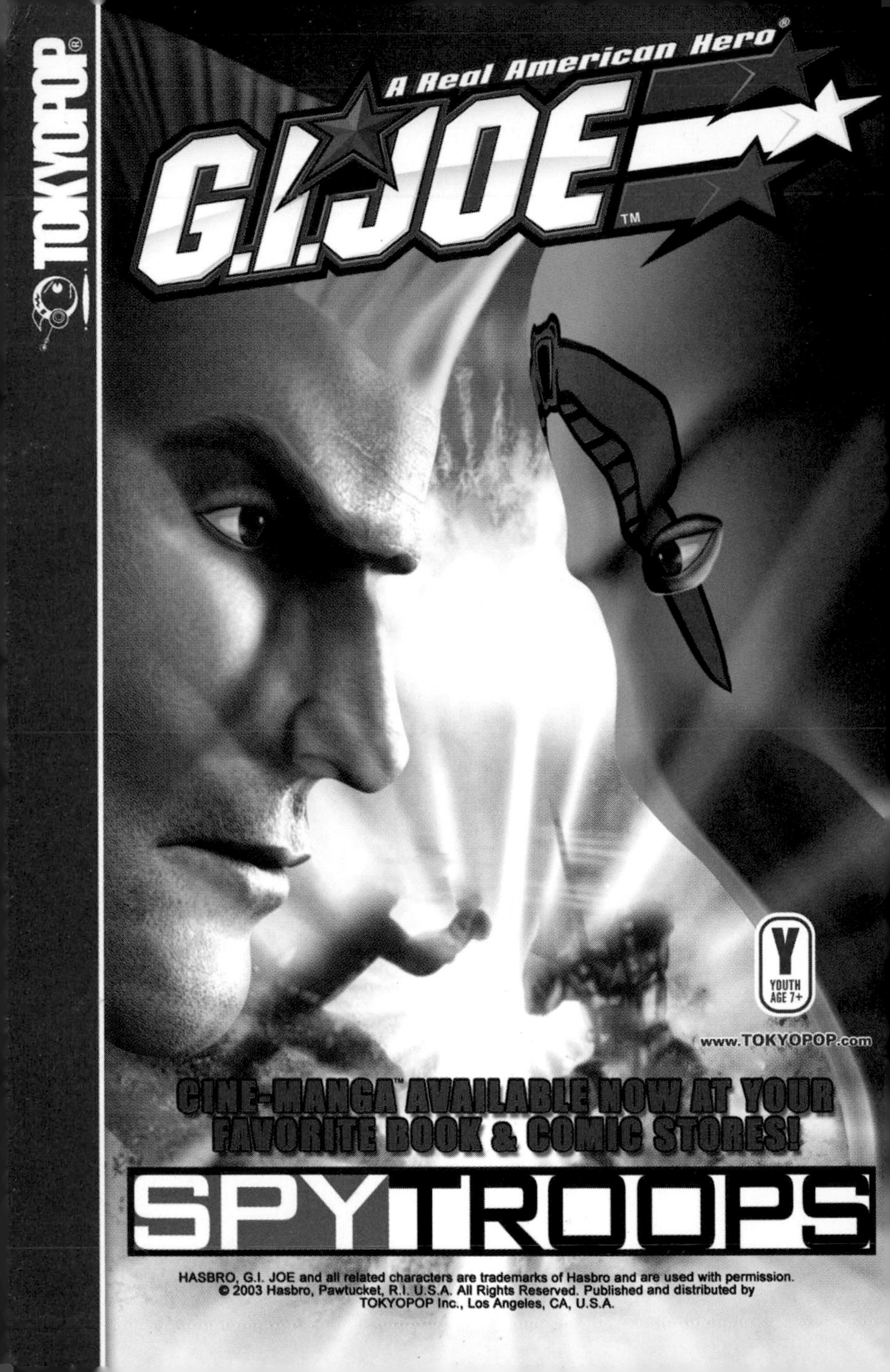
TOKYOPOP®
A Real American Hero®
G.I. JOE™
Y
YOUTH
AGE 7+
www.TOKYOPOP.com
CINE-MANGA™ AVAILABLE NOW AT YOUR
FAVORITE BOOK & COMIC STORES!
SPY TROOPS
HASBRO, G.I. JOE and all related characters are trademarks of Hasbro and are used with permission.
© 2003 Hasbro, Pawtucket, R.I. U.S.A. All Rights Reserved. Published and distributed by
TOKYOPOP Inc., Los Angeles, CA, U.S.A.